HYMNS TO THE NIGHT

Novalis

HYMNS TO THE NIGHT

In Translation

Novalis

Translated by George MacDonald, Henry Morley, M.J. Hope
and Paul B. Thomas

Edited by Carol Appleby

CRESCENT MOON

First published 2020.

Design by Radiance Graphics
Set in Bodoni Book 11 on 14pt.

British Library Cataloguing in Publication data available for this title.

ISBN-13 9781861717337 (Pbk)

Crescent Moon Publishing
P.O. Box 1312
Maidstone, Kent
ME14 5XU, Great Britain
www.crmoon.com

CONTENTS

NOTE ON THE TEXTS

Translated by George MacDonald.
From *Rampoli: Growths From a Long-planted Root* (1897) by George MacDonald, edited by Julian Hawthorne, and published by Longmans, Green, London, 1897.

Translated by Henry Morley (*circa* 1842).
From *Peter Schlemihl* by Adelbert Chiamasso, edited by Henry Morley, Cassell & Co., London, 1889.

Translated by M.J. Hope.
From *Novalis: His Life, Thoughts and Works* edited and translated by M.J. Hope, published by A.C. McClurg, Chicago, 1891.

Translated by Paul B. Thomas.
From *The German Classics: Masterpieces of German Literature* ed. Kuno Francke, 1914.

Novalis

Novalis

Hymnen an die Nacht

1

Welcher Lebendige, Sinnbegabte, liebt nicht vor allen Wunderer-
scheinungen des verbreiteten Raums um ihn, das allerfreuliche Licht
– mit seinen Farben, seinen Strahlen und Wogen; seiner milden
Allgegenwart, als weckender Tag. Wie des Lebens innerste Seele
atmet es der rastlosen Gestirne Riesenwelt, und schwimmt tanzend in
seiner blauen Flut – atmet es der funkelnde, ewigruhende Stein, die
sinnige, saugende Pflanze, und das wilde, brennende, vielgestaltete
Tier – vor allen aber der herrliche Fremdling mit den sinnvollen
Augen, dem schwebenden Gange, und den zartgeschlossenen,
tonreichen Lippen. Wie ein König der irdischen Natur ruft es jede
Kraft zu zahllosen Verwandlungen, knüpft und löst unendliche
Bündnisse, hängt sein himmlisches Bild jedem irdischen Wesen um. –
Seine Gegenwart allein offenbart die Wunderherrlichkeit der Reiche
der Welt.

Abwärts wend ich mich zu der heiligen, unaussprechlichen,
geheimnisvollen Nacht. Fernab liegt die Welt – in eine tiefe Gruft
versenkt – wüst und einsam ist ihre Stelle. In den Saiten der Brust
weht tiefe Wehmut. In Tautropfen will ich hinuntersinken und mit der
Asche mich vermischen. – Fernen der Erinnerung, Wünsche der
Jugend, der Kindheit Träume, des ganzen langen Lebens kurze
Freuden und vergebliche Hoffnungen kommen in grauen Kleidern,
wie Abendnebel nach der Sonne Untergang. In andern Räumen
schlug die lustigen Gezelte das Licht auf. Sollte es nie zu seinen
Kindern wiederkommen, die mit der Unschuld Glauben seiner
harren?

Was quillt auf einmal so ahndungsvoll unterm Herzen, und
verschluckt der Wehmut weiche Luft? Hast auch du ein Gefallen an
uns, dunkle Nacht? Was hältst du unter deinem Mantel, das mir
unsichtbar kräftig an die Seele geht? Köstlicher Balsam träuft aus
deiner Hand, aus dem Bündel Mohn. Die schweren Flügel des
Gemüts hebst du empor. Dunkel und unaussprechlich fühlen wir uns

bewegt – ein ernstes Antlitz seh ich froh erschrocken, das sanft und andachtsvoll sich zu mir neigt, und unter unendlich verschlungenen Locken der Mutter liebe Jugend zeigt. Wie arm und kindisch dünkt mir das Licht nun – wie erfreulich und gesegnet des Tages Abschied – Also nur darum, weil die Nacht dir abwendig macht die Dienenden, säetest du in des Raumes Weiten die leuchtenden Kugeln, zu verkünden deine Allmacht – deine Wiederkehr – in den Zeiten deiner Entfernung. Himmlischer, als jene blitzenden Sterne, dünken uns die unendlichen Augen, die die Nacht in uns geöffnet. Weiter sehn sie, als die blässesten jener zahllosen Heere – unbedürftig des Lichts durchschaun sie die Tiefen eines liebenden Gemüts – was einen höhern Raum mit unsäglicher Wollust füllt. Preis der Weltkönigin, der hohen Verkündigerin heiliger Welten, der Pflegerin seliger Liebe – sie sendet mir dich – zarte Geliebte – liebliche Sonne der Nacht, – nun wach ich – denn ich bin Dein und Mein – du hast die Nacht mir zum Leben verkündet – mich zum Menschen gemacht – zehre mit Geisterglut meinen Leib, daß ich luftig mit dir inniger mich mische und dann ewig die Brautnacht währt.

Muß immer der Morgen wiederkommen? Endet nie des Irdischen Gewalt? unselige Geschäftigkeit verzehrt den himmlischen Anflug der Nacht. Wird nie der Liebe geheimes Opfer ewig brennen? Zugemessen ward dem Lichte seine Zeit; aber zeitlos und raumlos ist der Nacht Herrschaft. – Ewig ist die Dauer des Schlafs. Heiliger Schlaf – beglücke zu selten nicht der Nacht Geweihte in diesem irdischen Tagewerk. Nur die Toren verkennen dich und wissen von keinem Schlafe, als den Schatten, den du in jener Dämmerung der wahrhaften Nacht mitleidig auf uns wirfst. Sie fühlen dich nicht in der goldnen Flut der Trauben – in des Mandelbaums Wunderöl, und dem braunen Safte des Mohns. Sie wissen nicht, daß du es bist der des zarten Mädchens Busen umschwebt und zum Himmel den Schoß macht – ahnden nicht, daß aus alten Geschichten du himmelöffnend entgegentrittst und den Schlüssel trägst zu den Wohnungen der Seligen, unendlicher Geheimnisse schweigender Bote.

Einst da ich bittre Tränen vergoß, da in Schmerz aufgelöst meine Hoffnung zerrann, und ich einsam stand am dürren Hügel, der in engen, dunkeln Raum die Gestalt meines Lebens barg – einsam, wie noch kein Einsamer war, von unsäglicher Angst getrieben – kraftlos, nur ein Gedanken des Elends noch. – Wie ich da nach Hülfe umherschaute, vorwärts nicht konnte und rückwärts nicht, und am fliehenden, verlöschten Leben mit unendlicher Sehnsucht hing: – da kam aus blauen Fernen – von den Höhen meiner alten Seligkeit ein Dämmerungsschauer – und mit einem Male riß das Band der Geburt – des Lichtes Fessel. Hin floh die irdische Herrlichkeit und meine Trauer mit ihr – zusammen floß die Wehmut in eine neue, unergründliche Welt – du Nachtbegeisterung, Schlummer des Himmels kamst über mich – die Gegend hob sich sacht empor; über der Gegend schwebte mein entbundner, neugeborner Geist. Zur Staubwolke wurde der Hügel – durch die Wolke sah ich die verklärten Züge der Geliebten. In ihren Augen ruhte die Ewigkeit – ich faßte ihre Hände, und die Tränen wurden ein funkelndes, unzerreißliches Band. Jahrtausende zogen abwärts in die Ferne, wie Ungewitter. An ihrem Halse weint ich dem neuen Leben entzückende Tränen. – Es war der erste, einzige Traum – und erst seitdem fühl ich ewigen, unwandelbaren Glauben an den Himmel der Nacht und sein Licht, die Geliebte.

4

Nun weiß ich, wenn der letzte Morgen sein wird – wenn das Licht
nicht mehr die Nacht und die Liebe scheucht – wenn der Schlummer
ewig und nur Ein unerschöpflicher Traum sein wird. Himmlische
Müdigkeit fühl ich in mir. – Weit und ermüdend ward mir die
Wallfahrt zum heiligen Grabe, drückend das Kreuz. Die kristallene
Woge, die gemeinen Sinnen unvernehmlich, in des Hügels dunkelm
Schoß quillt, an dessen Fuß die irdische Flut bricht, wer sie gekostet,
wer oben stand auf dem Grenzgebürge der Welt, und hinübersah in
das neue Land, in der Nacht Wohnsitz – wahrlich der kehrt nicht in
das Treiben der Welt zurück, in das Land, wo das Licht in ewiger
Unruh hauset.

Oben baut er sich Hütten, Hütten des Friedens, sehnt sich und liebt,
schaut hinüber, bis die willkommenste aller Stunden hinunter ihn in
den Brunnen der Quelle zieht – das Irdische schwimmt obenauf, wird
von Stürmen zurückgeführt, aber was heilig durch der Liebe
Berührung ward, rinnt aufgelöst in verborgenen Gängen auf das
jenseitige Gebiet, wo es, wie Düfte, sich mit entschlummerten Lieben
mischt. Noch weckst du, muntres Licht den Müden zur Arbeit – flößest
fröhliches Leben mir ein – aber du lockst mich von der Erinnerung
moosigem Denkmal nicht. Gern will ich die fleißigen Hände rühren,
überall umschaun, wo du mich brauchst – rühmen deines Glanzes
volle Pracht – unverdrossen verfolgen deines künstlichen Werks
schönen Zusammenhang – gern betrachten deiner gewaltigen,
leuchtenden Uhr sinnvollen Gang – ergründen der Kräfte Ebenmaß
und die Regeln des Wunderspiels unzähliger Räume und ihrer Zeiten.
Aber getreu der Nacht bleibt mein geheimes Herz, und der
schaffenden Liebe, ihrer Tochter. Kannst du mir zeigen ein ewig
treues Herz? hat deine Sonne freundliche Augen, die mich erkennen?
fassen deine Sterne meine verlangende Hand? Geben mir wieder den
zärtlichen Druck und das kosende Wort? Hast du mit Farben und
leichtem Umriß Sie geziert – oder war Sie es, die deinem Schmuck

höhere, liebere Bedeutung gab? Welche Wollust, welchen Genuß bietet dein Leben, die aufwögen des Todes Entzückungen? Trägt nicht alles, was uns begeistert, die Farbe der Nacht? Sie trägt dich mütterlich und ihr verdankst du all deine Herrlichkeit. Du verflögst in dir selbst – in endlosen Raum zergingst du, wenn sie dich nicht hielte, dich nicht bände, daß du warm würdest und flammend die Welt zeugtest. Wahrlich ich war, eh du warst – die Mutter schickte mit meinen Geschwistern mich, zu bewohnen deine Welt, sie zu heiligen mit Liebe, daß sie ein ewig angeschautes Denkmal werde – zu bepflanzen sie mit unverwelklichen Blumen. Noch reiften sie nicht diese göttlichen Gedanken – Noch sind der Spuren unserer Offenbarung wenig – Einst zeigt deine Uhr das Ende der Zeit, wenn du wirst wie unsereiner, und voll Sehnsucht und Inbrunst auslöschest und stirbst. In mir fühl ich deiner Geschäftigkeit Ende – himmlische Freiheit, selige Rückkehr. In wilden Schmerzen erkenn ich deine Entfernung von unsrer Heimat, deinen Widerstand gegen den alten, herrlichen Himmel. Deine Wut und dein Toben ist vergebens. Unverbrennlich steht das Kreuz – eine Siegesfahne unsers Geschlechts.

Hinüber wall ich,
Und jede Pein
Wird einst ein Stachel
Der Wollust sein.
Noch wenig Zeiten,
So bin ich los,
Und liege trunken
Der Lieb im Schoß.
Unendliches Leben
Wogt mächtig in mir
Ich schaue von oben
Herunter nach dir.
An jenem Hügel
Verlischt dein Glanz –
Ein Schatten bringet
Den kühlenden Kranz.
O! sauge, Geliebter,
Gewaltig mich an,
Daß ich entschlummern
Und lieben kann.
Ich fühle des Todes
Verjüngende Flut,
Zu Balsam und Äther
Verwandelt mein Blut –
Ich lebe bei Tage
Voll Glauben und Mut
Und sterbe die Nächte
In heiliger Glut.

Über der Menschen weitverbreitete Stämme herrschte vor Zeiten ein eisernes Schicksal mit stummer Gewalt. Eine dunkle, schwere Binde lag um ihre bange Seele – Unendlich war die Erde – der Götter Aufenthalt, und ihre Heimat. Seit Ewigkeiten stand ihr geheimnisvoller Bau. Über des Morgens roten Bergen, in des Meeres heiligem Schoß wohnte die Sonne, das allzündende, lebendige Licht. Ein alter Riese trug die selige Welt. Fest unter Bergen lagen die Ursöhne der Mutter Erde. Ohnmächtig in ihrer zerstörenden Wut gegen das neue herrliche Göttergeschlecht und dessen Verwandten, die fröhlichen Menschen. Des Meers dunkle, grüne Tiefe war einer Göttin Schoß. In den kristallenen Grotten schwelgte ein üppiges Volk. Flüsse, Bäume, Blumen und Tiere hatten menschlichen Sinn. Süßer schmeckte der Wein von sichtbarer Jugendfülle geschenkt – ein Gott in den Trauben – eine liebende, mütterliche Göttin, emporwachsend in vollen goldenen Garben – der Liebe heilger Rausch ein süßer Dienst der schönsten Götterfrau – ein ewig buntes Fest der Himmelskinder und der Erdbewohner rauschte das Leben, wie ein Frühling, durch die Jahrhunderte hin – Alle Geschlechter verehrten kindlich die zarte, tausendfältige Flamme, als das höchste der Welt. Ein Gedanke nur war es, Ein entsetzliches Traumbild,

Das furchtbar zu den frohen Tischen trat
Und das Gemüt in wilde Schrecken hüllte.
Hier wußten selbst die Götter keinen Rat
Der die beklommne Brust mit Trost erfüllte.
Geheimnisvoll war dieses Unholds Pfad
Des Wut kein Flehn und keine Gabe stillte;
Es war der Tod, der dieses Lustgelag
Mit Angst und Schmerz und Tränen unterbrach.
Auf ewig nun von allem abgeschieden,
Was hier das Herz in süßer Wollust regt,
Getrennt von den Geliebten, die hienieden
Vergebne Sehnsucht, langes Weh bewegt,
Schien matter Traum dem Toten nur beschieden,
Ohnmächtiges Ringen nur ihm auferlegt.
Zerbrochen war die Woge des Genusses
Am Felsen des unendlichen Verdrusses.
Mit kühnem Geist und hoher Sinnenglut
Verschönte sich der Mensch die grause Larve,
Ein sanfter Jüngling löscht das Licht und ruht –
Sanft wird das Ende, wie ein Wehn der Harfe.
Erinnerung schmilzt in kühler Schattenflut,
So sang das Lied dem traurigen Bedarfe.
Doch unenträtselt blieb die ewge Nacht,
Das ernste Zeichen einer fernen Macht.

Zu Ende neigte die alte Welt sich. Des jungen Geschlechts Lustgarten verwelkte – hinauf in den freieren, wüsten Raum strebten die unkindlichen, wachsenden Menschen. Die Götter verschwanden mit ihrem Gefolge – Einsam und leblos stand die Natur. Mit eiserner Kette band sie die dürre Zahl und das strenge Maß. Wie in Staub und Lüfte zerfiel in dunkle Worte die unermeßliche Blüte des Lebens. Entflohn war der beschwörende Glauben, und die allverwandelnde, allverschwisternde Himmelsgenossin, die Phantasie. Unfreundlich blies ein kalter Nordwind über die erstarrte Flur, und die erstarrte Wunderheimat verflog in den Äther. Des Himmels Fernen füllten mit leuchtenden Welten sich. Ins tiefre Heiligtum, in des Gemüts höhern Raum zog mit ihren Mächten die Seele der Welt – zu walten dort bis zum Anbruch der tagenden Weltherrlichkeit. Nicht mehr war das Licht der Götter Aufenthalt und himmlisches Zeichen – den Schleier der Nacht warfen sie über sich. Die Nacht ward der Offenbarungen mächtiger Schoß – in ihn kehrten die Götter zurück – schlummerten ein, um in neuen herrlichern Gestalten auszugehn über die veränderte Welt. Im Volk, das vor allen verachtet zu früh reif und der seligen Unschuld der Jugend trotzig fremd geworden war, erschien mit niegesehenem Angesicht die neue Welt – In der Armut dichterischer Hütte – Ein Sohn der ersten Jungfrau und Mutter – Geheimnisvoller Umarmung unendliche Frucht. Des Morgenlands ahndende, blütenreiche Weisheit erkannte zuerst der neuen Zeit Beginn – Zu des Königs demütiger Wiege wies ihr ein Stern den Weg. In der weiten Zukunft Namen huldigten sie ihm mit Glanz und Duft, den höchsten Wundern der Natur. Einsam entfaltete das himmlische Herz sich zu einem Blütenkelch allmächtger Liebe – des Vaters hohem Antlitz zugewandt und ruhend an dem ahndungsselgen Busen der lieblich ernsten Mutter. Mit vergötternder Inbrunst schaute das weissagende Auge des blühenden Kindes auf die Tage der Zukunft, nach seinen Geliebten, den Sprossen seines Götterstamms, unbekümmert über seiner Tage irdisches Schicksal. Bald sammelten die kindlichsten

Gemüter von inniger Liebe wundersam ergriffen sich um ihn her. Wie Blumen keimte ein neues fremdes Leben in seiner Nähe. Unerschöpfliche Worte und der Botschaften fröhlichste fielen wie Funken eines göttlichen Geistes von seinen freundlichen Lippen. Von ferner Küste, unter Hellas heiterm Himmel geboren, kam ein Sänger nach Palästina und ergab sein ganzes Herz dem Wunderkinde:

Der Jüngling bist du, der seit langer Zeit
Auf unsern Gräbern steht in tiefen Sinnen;
Ein tröstlich Zeichen in der Dunkelheit –
Der höhern Menschheit freudiges Beginnen.
Was uns gesenkt in tiefe Traurigkeit
Zieht uns mit süßer Sehnsucht nun von hinnen.
Im Tode ward das ewge Leben kund,
Du bist der Tod und machst uns erst gesund.

Der Sänger zog voll Freudigkeit nach Indostan – das Herz von süßer Liebe trunken; und schüttete in feurigen Gesängen es unter jenem milden Himmel aus, daß tausend Herzen sich zu ihm neigten, und die fröhliche Botschaft tausendzweigig emporwuchs. Bald nach des Sängers Abschied ward das köstliche Leben ein Opfer des menschlichen tiefen Verfalls – Er starb in jungen Jahren, weggerissen von der geliebten Welt, von der weinenden Mutter und seinen zagenden Freunden. Der unsäglichen Leiden dunkeln Kelch leerte der liebliche Mund – In entsetzlicher Angst nahte die Stunde der Geburt der neuen Welt. Hart rang er mit des alten Todes Schrecken – Schwer lag der Druck der alten Welt auf ihm. Noch einmal sah er freundlich nach der Mutter – da kam der ewigen Liebe lösende Hand – und er entschlief. Nur wenig Tage hing ein tiefer Schleier über das brausende Meer, über das bebende Land – unzählige Tränen weinten die Geliebten – Entsiegelt ward das Geheimnis – himmlische Geister hoben den uralten Stein vom dunkeln Grabe. Engel saßen bei dem Schlummernden – aus seinen Träumen zartgebildet – Erwacht in neuer Götterherrlichkeit erstieg er die Höhe der neugebornen Welt – begrub mit eigner Hand der Alten Leichnam in die verlaßne Höhle, und legte mit allmächtiger Hand den Stein, den keine Macht erhebt, darauf.

Noch weinen deine Lieben Tränen der Freude, Tränen der Rührung und des unendlichen Danks an deinem Grabe – sehn dich noch immer, freudig erschreckt, auferstehn – und sich mit dir; sehn dich weinen mit süßer Inbrunst an der Mutter seligem Busen, ernst mit den Freunden wandeln, Worte sagen, wie vom Baum des Lebens gebrochen; sehen dich eilen mit voller Sehnsucht in des Vaters Arm, bringend die junge Menschheit, und der goldnen Zukunft unversiglichen Becher. Die Mutter eilte bald dir nach – in himmlischem Triumph – Sie war die Erste in der neuen Heimat bei dir. Lange Zeiten entflossen seitdem, und in immer höherm Glanze regte deine neue Schöpfung sich – und Tausende zogen aus

Schmerzen und Qualen, voll Glauben und Sehnsucht und Treue dir nach – wallen mit dir und der himmlischen Jungfrau im Reiche der Liebe – dienen im Tempel des himmlischen Todes und sind in Ewigkeit dein.

Gehoben ist der Stein –
Die Menschheit ist erstanden –
Wir alle bleiben dein
Und fühlen keine Banden.
Der herbste Kummer fleucht
Vor deiner goldnen Schale,
Wenn Erd und Leben weicht,
Im letzten Abendmahle.
Zur Hochzeit ruft der Tod –
Die Lampen brennen helle –
Die Jungfraun sind zur Stelle
Um Öl ist keine Not –
Erklänge doch die Ferne
Von deinem Zuge schon,
Und ruften uns die Sterne
Mit Menschenzung und Ton.
Nach dir, Maria, heben
Schon tausend Herzen sich.
In diesem Schattenleben
Verlangten sie nur dich.
Sie hoffen zu genesen
Mit ahndungsvoller Lust –
Drückst du sie, heilges Wesen,
An deine treue Brust.
So manche, die sich glühend
In bittrer Qual verzehrt,
Und dieser Welt entfliehend
Nach dir sich hingekehrt;
Die hülfreich uns erschienen
In mancher Not und Pein –
Wir kommen nun zu ihnen
Um ewig da zu sein.

Nun weint an keinem Grabe,
Für Schmerz, wer liebend glaubt.
Der Liebe süße Habe
Wird keinem nicht geraubt –
Die Sehnsucht ihm zu lindern,
Begeistert ihn die Nacht –
Von treuen Himmelskindern
Wird ihm sein Herz bewacht.
Getrost, das Leben schreitet
Zum ewgen Leben hin;
Von innrer Glut geweitet
Verklärt sich unser Sinn.
Die Sternwelt wird zerfließen
Zum goldnen Lebenswein,
Wir werden sie genießen
Und lichte Sterne sein.
Die Lieb ist frei gegeben,
und keine Trennung mehr.
Es wogt das volle Leben
Wie ein unendlich Meer.
Nur Eine Nacht der Wonne –
Ein ewiges Gedicht –
Und unser aller Sonne
Ist Gottes Angesicht.

6

Sehnsucht nach dem Tode
Hinunter in der Erde Schoß,
Weg aus des Lichtes Reichen,
Der Schmerzen Wut und wilder Stoß
Ist froher Abfahrt Zeichen.
Wir kommen in dem engen Kahn
Geschwind am Himmelsufer an.
Gelobt sei uns die ewge Nacht,
Gelobt der ewge Schlummer.
Wohl hat der Tag uns warm gemacht,
Und welk der lange Kummer.
Die Lust der Fremde ging uns aus,
Zum Vater wollen wir nach Haus.
Was sollen wir auf dieser Welt
Mit unsrer Lieb und Treue.
Das Alte wird hintangestellt,
Was soll uns dann das Neue.
O! einsam steht und tiefbetrübt,
Wer heiß und fromm die Vorzeit liebt.
Die Vorzeit wo die Sinne licht
In hohen Flammen brannten,
Des Vaters Hand und Angesicht
Die Menschen noch erkannten.
Und hohen Sinns, einfältiglich
Noch mancher seinem Urbild glich.
Die Vorzeit, wo noch blütenreich
Uralte Stämme prangten,
Und Kinder für das Himmelreich
Nach Qual und Tod verlangten.
Und wenn auch Lust und Leben sprach
Doch manches Herz für Liebe brach.

Die Vorzeit, wo in Jugendglut
Gott selbst sich kundgegeben
Und frühem Tod in Liebesmut
Geweiht sein süßes Leben.
Und Angst und Schmerz nicht von sich trieb,
Damit er uns nur teuer blieb.
Mit banger Sehnsucht sehn wir sie
In dunkle Nacht gehüllet,
In dieser Zeitlichkeit wird nie
Der heiße Durst gestillet.
Wir müssen nach der Heimat gehn,
Um diese heilge Zeit zu sehn.
Was hält noch unsre Rückkehr auf,
Die Liebsten ruhn schon lange.
Ihr Grab schließt unsern Lebenslauf,
Nun wird uns weh und bange.
Zu suchen haben wir nichts mehr –
Das Herz ist satt – die Welt ist leer.
Unendlich und geheimnisvoll
Durchströmt uns süßer Schauer –
Mir däucht, aus tiefen Fernen scholl
Ein Echo unsrer Trauer.
Die Lieben sehnen sich wohl auch
Und sandten uns der Sehnsucht Hauch.
Hinunter zu der süßen Braut,
Zu Jesus, dem Geliebten –
Getrost, die Abenddämmrung graut
Den Liebenden, Betrübten.
Ein Traum bricht unsre Banden los
Und senkt uns in des Vaters Schoß.

Hymns To the Night

Translated by George MacDonald[1]

1 From *Rampoli: Growths From a Long-planted Root* (1897) by George MacDonald, edited by Julian Hawthorne, and published by Longmans, Green, London, 1897.

1

Before all the wondrous shows of the widespread space around him, what living, sentient thing loves not the all-joyous light, with its colors, its rays and undulations, its gentle omnipresence in the form of the wakening Day? The giant-world of the unresting constellations inhales it as the innermost soul of life, and floats dancing in its azure flood; the sparkling, ever-tranquil stone, the thoughtful, imbibing plant, and the wild, burning multiform beast inhales it; but more than all, the lordly stranger with the sense-filled eyes, the swaying walk, and the sweetly closed, melodious lips. Like a king over earthly nature, it rouses every force to countless transformations, binds and unbinds innumerable alliances, hangs its heavenly form around every earthly substance. Its presence alone reveals the marvelous splendor of the kingdoms of the world.

Aside I turn to the holy, unspeakable, mysterious Night. Afar lies the world, sunk in a deep grave; waste and lonely is its place. In the chords of the bosom blows a deep sadness. I am ready to sink away in drops of dew, and mingle with the ashes. – The distances of memory, the wishes of youth, the dreams of childhood, the brief joys and vain hopes of a whole long life, arise in gray garments, like an evening vapor after the sunset. In other regions the light has pitched its joyous tents. What if it should never return to its children, who wait for it with the faith of innocence?

What springs up all at once so sweetly boding in my heart, and stills the soft air of sadness? Dost thou also take a pleasure in us, dark Night? What holdest thou under thy mantle, that with hidden power affects my soul? Precious balm drips from thy hand out of its bundle of poppies. Thou upliftest the heavy-laden wings of the soul. Darkly and inexpressibly are we moved: joy-startled, I see a grave face that, tender and worshipful, inclines toward me, and, amid manifold entangled locks, reveals the youthful loveliness of the Mother. How poor and childish a thing seems to me now the Light!

how joyous and welcome the departure of the day! – Didst thou not only therefore, because the Night turns away from thee thy servants, you now strew in the gulfs of space those flashing globes, to proclaim, in seasons of thy absence, thy omnipotence, and thy return?

More heavenly than those glittering stars we hold the eternal eyes which the Night hath opened within us. Farther they see than the palest of those countless hosts. Needing no aid from the light, they penetrate the depths of a loving soul that fills a loftier region with bliss ineffable. Glory to the queen of the world, to the great prophet of the holier worlds, to the guardian of blissful love! she sends thee to me, thou tenderly beloved, the gracious sun of the Night. Now am I awake, for now am I thine and mine. Thou hast made me know the Night, and brought her to me to be my life; thou hast made of me a man. Consume my body with the ardour of my soul, that I, turned to finer air, may mingle more closely with thee, and then our bridal night endure for ever.

2

Must the morning always return? Will the despotism of the earthly never cease? Unholy activity consumes the angel-visit of the Night. Will the time never come when Love's hidden sacrifice shall burn eternally? To the Light a season was set; but everlasting and boundless is the dominion of the Night. Endless is the duration of sleep. Holy Sleep, gladden not too seldom in this earthly day-labor, the devoted servant of the Night. Fools alone mistake thee, knowing nought of sleep but the shadow which, in the twilight of the real Night, thou pitifully castest over us. They feel thee not in the golden flood of the grapes, in the magic oil of the almond tree, and the brown juice of the poppy. They know not that it is thou who hauntest the bosom of the tender maiden, and makest a heaven of her lap; never suspect it is thou, opening the doors to Heaven, that steppest to meet them out of ancient stories, bearing the key to the dwellings of the blessed, silent messenger of secrets infinite.

3

Once when I was shedding bitter tears, when, dissolved in pain, my hope was melting away, and I stood alone by the barren mound which in its narrow dark bosom hid the vanished form of my Life, lonely as never yet was lonely man, driven by anxiety unspeakable, powerless, and no longer anything but a conscious misery; – as there I looked about me for help, unable to go on or to turn back, and clung to the fleeting, extinguished life with an endless longing: then, out of the blue distances – from the hills of my ancient bliss, came a shiver of twilight – and at once snapt the bond of birth, the chains of the Light. Away fled the glory of the world, and with it my mourning; the sadness flowed together into a new, unfathomable world. Thou, soul of the Night, heavenly Slumber, didst come upon me; the region gently upheaved itself; over it hovered my unbound, newborn spirit. The mound became a cloud of dust, and through the cloud I saw the glorified face of my beloved. In her eyes eternity reposed. I laid hold of her hands, and the tears became a sparkling bond that could not be broken. Into the distance swept by, like a tempest, thousands of years. On her neck I welcomed the new life with ecstatic tears. Never was was such another dream; then first and ever since I hold fast an eternal, unchangeable faith in the heaven of the Night, and its Light, the Beloved.

4

Now I know when will come the last morning: when the Light no more scares away the Night and Love, when sleep shall be without waking, and but one continuous dream. I feel in me a celestial exhaustion. Long and weariful was my pilgrimage to the holy grave, and crushing was the cross. The crystal wave, which, imperceptible to the ordinary sense, springs in the dark bosom of the mound against whose foot breaks the flood of the world, he who has tasted it, he who has stood on the mountain frontier of the world, and looked across into the new land, into the abode of the Night, verily he turns not again into the tumult of the world, into the land where dwells the Light in ceaseless unrest. On those heights he builds for himself tabernacles – tabernacles of peace; there longs and loves and gazes across, until the welcomest of all hours draws him down into the waters of the spring. Afloat above remains what is earthly, and is swept back in storms; but what became holy by the touch of Love, runs free through hidden ways to the region beyond, where, like odours, it mingles with love asleep. Still wakest thou, cheerful Light, that weary man to his labour, and into me pourest gladsome life; but thou wilest me not away from Memory's moss-grown monument. Gladly will I stir busy hands, everywhere behold where thou hast need of me; bepraise the rich pomp of thy splendor; pursue unwearied the lovely harmonies of thy skilled handicraft; gladly contemplate the clever pace of thy mighty, radiant clock; explore the balance of the forces and the laws of the wondrous play of countless worlds and their seasons; but true to the Night remains my secret heart, and to creative Love, her daughter. Canst *thou* show me a heart eternally true? Has thy sun friendly eyes that know me? Do thy stars lay hold of my longing hand? Do they return me the tender pressure and the caressing word? Was it thou did bedeck them with colours and a flickering outline? Or was it *she* who gave to thy jewels a higher, a dearer significance? What delight, what pleasure offers *thy* life, to outweigh the transports of Death? Wears not everything that inspirits us the livery of the Night? Thy mother, it is she brings thee forth, and to her thou owest all thy glory. Thou wouldst vanish into thyself, thou wouldst dissipate in boundless space, if she did not hold thee fast, if she swaddled thee not, so that thou grewest warm, and flaming, gavest birth to the universe. Verily I was before thou wast; the mother sent me with sisters to inhabit thy world, to sanctify it with love that it might be an ever-present memorial, to plant it with flowers unfading. As yet they have not ripened, these thoughts divine; as yet is there small trace of our coming apocalypse. One day thy clock will point to the end of Time, and then thou shalt be as one of us, and shalt, full of ardent longing, be extinguished and die. I feel in me the close of thy activity, I taste heavenly freedom, and happy restoration. With wild pangs I recognize thy distance from our home, thy feud with the ancient, glorious Heaven. Thy rage and thy raving are in vain. Inconsumable stands the cross, victory-flag of our race.

Over I pilgrim
Where every pain
Zest only of pleasure
Shall one day remain.
Yet a few moments
Then free am I,
And intoxicated
In Love's lap lie.
Life everlasting
Lifts, wave-like, at me:
I gaze from its summit
Down after thee.
Oh Sun, thou must vanish
Yon yon hillock beneath;
A shadow will bring thee
Thy cooling wreath.
Oh draw at my heart, love,
Draw till I'm gone,
That, fallen asleep, I
Still may love on.
I feel the flow of
Death's youth-giving flood;
To balsam and æther, it
Changes my blood!
I live all the daytime
In faith and in might:
And in holy rapture
I die every night.

5

In ancient times an iron Fate lorded it, with dumb force, over the widespread families of men. A gloomy oppression swathed their anxious souls: the earth was boundless, the abode of the gods and their home. From eternal ages stood its mysterious structure. Beyond the red hills of the morning, in the sacred bosom of the sea, dwelt the sun, the all-enkindling, live luminary. An aged giant upbore the happy world. Prisoned beneath mountains lay the first-born sons of mother Earth, helpless in their destroying fury against the new, glorious race of gods, and their kindred, glad-hearted men. Ocean's dusky, green abyss was the lap of a goddess. In the crystal grottos revelled a wanton folk. Rivers, trees, flowers, and beasts had human wits. Sweeter tasted the wine, poured out by Youth impersonated; a god was in the grape-clusters; a loving, motherly goddess upgrew in the full golden sheaves; love's sacred carousal was a sweet worship of the fairest of the goddesses. Life revelled through the centuries like one spring-time, an ever-variegated festival of the children of and the dewllers on the earth. All races childlike adored the ethereal, thousand-fold flame as the one sublimest thing in the world.

It was but a fancy, a horrible dream-shape —
That fearsome to the merry tables strode,
And wrapt the spirit in wild consternation.
The gods themselves here counsel knew nor showed
To fill the stifling heart with consolation.
Mysterious was the monster's pathless road,
Whose rage would heed no prayer and no oblation;
'Twas Death who broke the banquet up with fears,
With anguish, with dire pain, and bitter tears.
Eternally from all things here disparted
That sway the heart with pleasure's joyous flow,
Divided from the loved, whom, broken-hearted,
Vain longing tosses and unceasing woe —
In a dull dream to struggle, faint and thwarted,
Seemed all was granted to the dead below!
Broke lay the merry wave of human glory
On Death's inevitable promontory.
With daring flight, aloft Thoughts pinions sweep;,
The horrid thing with beauty'ss robe men cover:
A gentle youth puts out his torch, to sleep;
Sweet comes the end, like moaning lute of lover.
Cool shadow-floods o'er melting memory creep:
So sang the song, for Misery was the mover.
Still undeciphered lay the endless Night —
The solemn symbol of a far-off Might.

The old world began to decline. The pleasure-garden of the young race withered away; up into opener, regions and desolate, forsaking his childhood, struggled the growing man. The gods vanished with their retinue. Nature stood alone and lifeless. Dry Number and rigid Measure bound her with iron chains. As into dust and air the priceless blossoms of life fell away in words obscure. Gone was wonder-working Faith, and its all-transforming, all-uniting angel-comrade, the Imagination. A cold north wind blew unkindly over the torpid plain, and the wonderland first froze, then evaporated into æther. The far depths of heaven filled with flashing worlds. Into the deeper sanctuary, into the more exalted region of the mind, the soul of the world retired with all her powers, there to rule until the dawn should break of the glory universal. No longer was the Light the abode of the gods, and the heavenly token of their presence: they cast over them the veil of the Night. The Night became the mighty womb of revelations; into it the gods went back, and fell asleep, to go abroad in new and more glorious shapes over the transfigured world. Among the people which, untimely ripe, was become of all the most scornful and insolently hostile to the blessed innocence of youth, appeared the New World, in guise never seen before, in the song-favouring hut of poverty, a son of the first maid and mother, the eternal fruit of mysterious embrace. The foreseeing, rich-blossoming wisdom of the East at once recognized the beginning of the new age; a star showed it the way to the lowly cradle of the king. In the name of the far-reaching future, they did him homage with lustre and odour, the highest wonders of Nature. In solitude the heavenly heart unfolded itelf to a flower-chalice of almighty love, upturned to the supreme face of the father, and resting on the bliss-boding bosom of the sweetly solemn mother. With deifying fervour the prophetic eye of the blooming child beheld the years to come, foresaw, untroubled over the earthly lot of his own days, the beloved offspring of his divine stem. Ere long the most childlike souls, by true love marvellously possessed, gathered about him. Like flowers sprang up a strange new life in his presence. Words inexhaustible and the most joyful fell like sparks of a divine spirit from his friendly lips. From a far shore, came a singer, born under the clear sky of Hellas, to Palestine, and gave up his whole heart to the marvellous child:-

The youth thou art who ages long hast stood
Upon our graves, lost in am aze of weening;
Sign in the darkness of God's tidings good,
Whence hints og growth humanity is gleaning;
For that we long, on that we sweetly brood
Which erst in woe had lost all life and meaning;
In everlasting life death found its goal,
For thou art Death who at last mak'st us whole.

Filled with joy, the singer went on to Indostan, his heart intoxicated with the sweetest love, and poured it out in fiery songs under that tender sky, so that a thousand hearts bowed to him, and the good news sprang up with a thousand branches. Soon after the singer's departure, his precious life was made a sacrifice for the deep fall of man. He died in his youth, torn away from his loved world, from his weeping mother, and his trembling friends. His lovely mouth emptied the dark cup of unspeakable wrongs. In horrible anguish the birth of the new world drew near. Hard he wrestled with the terrors of old Death; heavy lay the weight of the old world upon him. Yet once more he looked kindly at his mother; then came the releasing hand of the Love eternal, and he fell asleep. Only a few days hung a deep veil over the roaring sea, over the quaking land; countless tears wept his loved ones; the mystery was unsealed: heavenly spirits heaved the ancient stone from the gloomy grave. Angels sat by the sleeper, sweetly outbodied from his dreams; awaked in new Godlike glory, he clomb the limits of the new-born world, buried with his own hand the old corpse in the forsaken cavity, and with hand almighty laid upon it the stone which no power shall again upheave.

Yet weep thy loved ones over thy grave tears of joy, tears of emotion, tears of endless thanksgiving; ever afresh with joyous start, they see thee rise again, and themselves with thee; behold thee weep with soft fervour on the blessed bosom of thy mother, walk in thoughtful communion with thy friends, uttering words plucked as from the tree of life; see thee hasten, full of longing, into thy father's arms, bearing with thee youthful Humanity, and the inexhaustible cup of the golden Future. Soon the mother hastened after thee in heavenly triumph; she was the first with thee in the new home. Since then, long ages have flowed past, and in splendour ever-increasing have bestirred thy new creation, and thousands have, out of pangs and tortures, followed thee, filled with faith and longing and truth, and are walking about with thee and the heavenly virgin in the kingdom of Love, minister in the temple of heavenly Death, and forever thine.

Uplifted is the stone,
And all mankind is risen;
We all remain thine own.
And vanished is our prison.
All troubles flee away
Before thy golden cup;
For Earth nor Life can stay
When with our Lord we sup.
To the marriage Death doth call;
No virgin holdeth back;
The lamps burn lustrous all;
Of oil there is no lack.
Would thy far feet were waking
The echoes of our street!
And that the stars were making
Signal with voices sweet.
To thee, O mother maiden
Ten thousand hearts aspire;
In this life, sorrow-laden,
Thee only they desire.
In thee they hope for healing;
In thee expect true rest,
When thou, their safety sealing,
Shalt clasp them to thy breast.
With disappointment burning
Who made in hell their bed,
At last from this world turning
To thee have looked and fled:
Helpful thou hast appeared
To us in many a pain:
Now to thy home we've neared,
Not to go out again!

Now at no grave are weeping
Such as do love and pray;
The gift that Love is keeping
From none is taken away.
To soothe and quiet our longing,
Night comes, and stills the smart;
Heaven's children round us thronging
Watch and ward our heart.
Courage! for life is striding
To endless life along;
The sense in love abiding,
Grows clearer and more strong.
One day the stars, down dripping,
Shall flow in golden wine:
We, of that nectar sipping,
As living stars will shine.
Free, from the tomb emerges
Love, to die never more;
Fulfilled, life heaves and surges
A sea without a shore.
All night! all blissful leisure!
One jubilating ode!
And the sun of all our pleasure
The countenance of God.

6

Longing for Death
Into the bosom of the earth!
Out of the Light's dominions!
Death's pains are but the bursting forth
Of glad departures pinions!
Swift in the narrow little boat,
Swift to the heavenly shore we float!
Blest be the everlasting Night,
And blest the endless slumber!
We are heated with the day too bright,
And withered up with cumber!
We're weary of that life abroad:
Come, we will now go home to God!
Why longer in this world abide?
Why love and truth here cherish?
That which is old is set aside –
For us the new may perish!
Alone he stands and sore downcast
Who loves with pious warmth the Past.
The Past where yet the human spirit
In lofty flames did rise;
Where men the Father did inherit,
His countenance recognize;
And, in simplicity made ripe,
Many grew like their archetype.
The Past wherein, still rich in bloom
Old stems did burgeon glorious;
And children, for the world to come,
Sought pain and death victorious;
And, through both life and pleasure spake,
Yet many a heart for love did break.

The Past, where to the flow of youth
God yet himself declared;
And early death in loving truth
The young beheld, and dared –
Anguish and torture parient bore
To prove they loved him as of yore
With anxious yearning now we see
That Past in darkness drenched;
With this world's water never we
Shall find our hot thirst quenched:
To our old home we have to go
That blessed time again to know.
What yet doth hinder our return?
Long since repose our precious!
Their grave is of our life the bourne;
We shrink from times ungracious!
By not a hope are we decoyed:
The heart is full; the world is void.
Infinite and mysterious,
Thrills through me a sweet trembling,
As if from far there echoed thus
A sigh, our grief resembling:
The dear ones long as well as I,
And sent to me their waiting sigh.
Down to the sweet bride, and away
To the beloved Jesus!
Courage! the evening shades grow gray,
Of all our griefs to ease us!
A dream will dash our chains apart,
And lay us on the Father's heart.

Novalis

Novalis

Sophie von Kühn

HYMNS TO THE NIGHT

Translated by Henry Morley[1]

1 Translated by Henry Morley *circa* 1842. From *Peter Schlemihl* by Adelbert Chiamasso, edited by Henry Morley, Cassell & Co., London, 1889.

I

Who that has life and intelligence, loves not, before all the surrounding miracles of space, ever-joyous light with its tints, its beams, and its waves, its mild omnipresence, when it comes as the waking day. Like the inmost soul of life, it is inhaled by the giant universe of gleaming stars, that dance as they swim in its blue flood; it is inhaled by the glittering, eternally motionless stone, by the living plant that drinks it in, by the wild and impetuous beast in its many forms; but above all, by the glorious stranger, with eyes of intellect, majestic step, with lips melodious, and gently closed. As a king over earthly nature, it calls forth to countless changes every power, binds and loosens bonds unnumbered, and hangs around every earthly being its heavenly picture. Alone its presence declares the wondrous glory of the kingdoms of the world.

I turn aside to the holy, the inexpressible, the mysterious Night. Afar off lies the world, buried in some deep chasm: desolate and lonely is the spot it filled. Through the chords of the breast sighs deepest sorrow. I will sink down into the dewdrops, and with ashes will I be commingled. The distant lines of memory, desires of youth, the dreams of childhood, a whole life's short joys and hopes vain, unfulfilled, come clothed in grey, like evening mists, when the sun's glory has departed. Elsewhere has the light broken upon habitations of gladness. What, should it never return again to its children, who with the faith of innocence await its coming?

What fount is thus suddenly opened within the heart, so full of forethought, that destroys the soft breath of sorrow? Thou also – dost thou love us, gloomy Night? What holdest thou concealed beneath thy mantle that draws my soul towards thee with such mysterious power? Costly balsam raineth from thy hand; from thy horn pourest thou out manna; the heavy wings of the spirit liftest thou. Darkly and inexpressibly do we feel ourselves moved: a solemn countenance I behold with glad alarm, that bends towards me in gentle contemplation, displaying, among endless allurements of the mother, lovely youth! How poor and childish does the light now seem! How joyous and how hallowed is the day's departure! – Therefore then only, because Night dismissed thy vassals, hast thou sown in the infinity of space those shining balls to declare thine almighty power, and thy return in the season of absence? More heavenly than those glittering stars seem the unnumbered eyes that Night has opened within us. Farther can they see than beyond the palest of that countless host; without need of light can they pierce the depths of a spirit of love, that fills a yet more glorious space with joy beyond expression. Glory to the world's Queen, the high declarer of spheres of holiness, the nurse of hallowed love! Thee, thou tenderly beloved one, doth she send to me – thee, lovely sun of the Night. Now I awaken, for I am thine and mine: the Night hast thou given as a sign of life, and made me man. Devour with glowing spiritual fire this earthly body, that I ethereal may abide with thee in union yet more perfect, and then may the bridal Night endure for ever.

II

Must ever the morn return? Is there no end to the sovereignty of earth? Unhallowed occupation breaks the heavenly pinion of the Night. Shall the secret offering of love at no time burn for ever? To the Light is its period allotted; but beyond time and space is the empire of the Night. Eternal is the duration of sleep. Thou holy sleep! bless not too rarely the Night's dedicated son in this earth's daily work! Fools alone recognise thee not, and know of no sleep beyond the shadow which in that twilight of the actual Night thou throwest in compassion over us. They feel thee not in the vine's golden flood, in the almond-tree's marvel oil, and in the brown juice of the manna; they know not that it is thou that enhaloest the tender maiden's breast, and makest a heaven of her bosom; conceive not that out of histories of old thou steppest forth an opener of heaven, and bearest the key to the abodes of the blessed, the silent messenger of unending mysteries.

III

Once, when I was shedding bitter tears, when my hope streamed away dissolved in sorrow, and I stood alone beside the barren hill, that concealed in narrow gloomy space the form of my existence – alone, as never solitary yet hath been, urged by an agony beyond expression, powerless, no more than a mere thought of sorrow; as I looked around me there for aid, could not advance, could not retire, and hung with incessant longing upon fleeting, failing life; – then came there from the blue distance, from the heights of my former happiness, a thin veil of the twilight gloom, and in a moment burst the bondage of the fetters of the birth of light. Then fled the glories of the earth, and all my sorrow with them; sadness melted away in a new, an unfathomable world; thou, inspiration of the Night, slumber of heaven, camest over me; the spot whereon I stood rose insensibly on high; above the spot soared forth my released and new-born spirit. The hill became a cloud of dust; through the cloud I beheld the revealed features of my beloved one. In her eyes eternity reposed; I grasped her hands, and my tears formed a glittering, inseparable bond. Ages were swept by like storms into the distance; on her neck I wept tears of ecstasy for life renewed. It was my first, my only dream; and from that time I feel an eternal and unchanging faith in the heaven of the Night, and in its light, the Loved One.

IV

Now do I know when the last morn will be; when the light shall no more give alarm to the night and to love; when the slumber shall be without end, and there shall be but one exhaustless dream. Heavenly weariness do I feel within me. Long and wearisome had become the pilgrimage to the holy grave – the cross a burthen. He who hath tasted of the crystal wave that gushes forth, unknown to common eye, in the dark bosom of that hill, against whose foot the flood of earthly waves is dashed and broken; he who hath stood upon the summit of the world's mountain bounds, and hath looked beyond them down into that new land, into the abode of Night; he, well I ween, turns not back into the turmoil of the world – into the land where the light, and eternal unrest, dwells.

There, above, does he erect his huts – his huts of peace; there longs and loves, until comes the most welcome of all hours to draw him down into that fountain's source. Upon the surface floats all that is earthly – it is hurried back by storms; but that which was hallowed by the breath of love, freely streams it forth, through hidden paths, into that realm beyond the mountain chain, and there, exhaled as incense, becomes mixed with loves that have slept. Still, cheerful light, dost thou waken the weary to his toil, still pourest thou glad life into my breast; but from the mossy monument that memory has raised, thence canst thou not allure me. Willingly will I employ my hands in industry and toil; I will look around me at thy bidding; I will celebrate the full glory of thy splendour; trace out, untired, the beauteous consistency of thy wondrous work; willingly will I mark the marvellous course of thy mighty, glowing timepiece; observe the balance of gigantic powers, and the laws of the wondrous play of countless spaces and their periods. But true to the Night remains my heart of hearts, and to creative Love, her daughter. Canst thou show me a heart for ever faithful? Hath thy sun fond eyes that know me? Do thy stars clasp my proffered hand? Do they return the tender pressure, the caressing word? Hast thou clothed her with fair hues and pleasing outline? Or was it she who gave thine ornament a higher, dearer meaning? What pleasure, what enjoyment, can thy life afford, that shall overweigh the ecstasies of death? Bears not everything that inspires us the colours of the Night? Thee she cherishes with a mother's care; to her thou owest all thy majesty. Thou hadst melted in thyself, hadst been dissolved in endless space, had she not restrained and encircled thee, so that thou wert warm, and gavest life to the world. Verily I was, before thou wert: the mother sent me with my sisters to inhabit thy world, to hallow it with love, so that it might be gazed on as a memorial for ever, to plant it with unfading flowers. As yet they have borne no fruit, these godlike thoughts; but few as yet are the traces of our revelation. The day shall come when thy timepiece pointeth to the end of time, when thou shalt be even as one of us; and, filled with longing and ardent love, be blotted out and die. Within my soul I feel the end of thy distracted power, heavenly freedom, hailed return. In wild sorrow I recognise thy distance from our home, thy hostility towards the ancient glorious heaven. In vain are thy tumult and thy rage. Indestructible remains the cross – a victorious banner of our race.

"I wander over,
       And every tear
To gem our pleasure
       Will then appear.
A few more hours,
       And I find my rest
In maddening bliss,
       On the loved one's breast.
Life, never ending,
       Swells mighty in me;
I look from above down –
       Look back upon thee.
By yonder hillock
       Expires thy beam;
And comes with a shadow,
       The cooling gleam.
Oh, call me, thou loved one,
       With strength from above;
That I may slumber,
       And wake to love.
I welcome death's
       Reviving flood;
To balm and to ether
       It changes my blood.
I live through each day,
       Filled with faith and desire;
And die when the Night comes
       In heaven-born fire."

V

Over the widely-spreading races of mankind, ruled aforetime an iron Destiny with silent power. A dark and heavy band was around man's anxious soul; without end was the earth; the home of the gods and their abode. Throughout eternities had her mysterious structure stood. Beyond the red mountains of the morning, in the holy bosom of the sea, there dwelt the Sun, the all-inflaming, living light. A hoary giant bare the sacred world. Securely prisoned, beneath mountains, lay the first sons of the mother Earth, powerless in their destructive fury against the new and glorious race of the gods, and their kindred, joyous men. The dark, green ocean's depth was the bosom of a goddess. In the crystal grottoes rioted a voluptuous tribe. Rivers, trees, flowers, and brute beasts had human understanding. Sweeter was the wine poured forth by youth's soft bloom; a god in the vine's clusters; a loving, a maternal goddess, shooting forth among the full, golden sheaves; love's holy flame, a delicious service to the most beauteous of the goddesses. An ever gay and joyous festival of heaven's children and the dwellers upon earth, life rustled on as a spring, through centuries. All races venerated, like children, the tender, thousand-fold flame, as the highest of the world; one thought only was there, one hideous vision of a dream: —

"That fearful to the joyous tables came,
   And the gay soul in wild distraction shrouded.
Here could the gods themselves no counsel frame,
   That might console the breast with sorrow clouded.
This monster's path mysterious, still the same,
   Unstilled his rage, though prayers on gifts were
                                        crowded.
His name was Death, who with distress of soul,
Anguish and tears, on the hour of pleasure stole.

For ever now from everything departed
   That here can swell the heart with sweet delight,
Torn now from the beloved one, who, sad-hearted,
   On earth could but desire and grief excite,
A feeble dream seemed to the dead imparted,
   Powerless striving made man's only right;
And broken was enjoyment's heaving billow,
Upon the rock of endless care, its pillow.

With daring mind, as heavenly fancy glows,
   Man masks the fearful shape with fair resembling:
His torch put out, a mild youth doth repose;
   Soft is the end as the lyre's mournful trembling.
Remembrance fades i' the gloom a shadow throws:
   So sang the song, a dreadful doom dissembling.
Yet undefined remained eternal Night,
The stern reminder of some distant might."

At length the old world bowed its head. The gay gardens of the young race were withered; beyond into the freer, desert space aspired less childish and maturing man. The gods then vanished with their train. Lonely and lifeless, Nature stood. The scanty number and the rigid measure bound her with fetters of iron. As into dust and air melted the inconceivable blossoms of life into mysterious words. Fled was the magic faith, and phantasy the all-changing, all-uniting friend from heaven. Over the rigid earth, unfriendly, blew a cold north wind, and the wonder-home, now without life, was lost in ether; the recesses of the heavens were filled with beaming worlds. Into a holier sphere, into the mind's far higher space, did the world draw the soul with its powers, there to wander until the break of the world's dawning glory. No longer was the light the gods' abode, their token in the heavens: the veil of the night did they cast over them. The night was the mighty bosom of revelations; in it the gods returned, and slumbered there, to go forth in new and in more glorious forms over the altered world.

Among the people above all despised, too soon matured, and wilful strangers to the blessed innocence of youth; among them, with features hitherto unseen, the new world came, in the poet's hut of poverty, a son of the first virgin mother, endless fruit of a mysterious embrace. The boding, budding wisdom of the East first recognised another Time's beginning; to the humble cradle of the monarch their star declared the way. In the name of the distant future, with splendour and with incense, did they make offering to him, the highest wonder of the world. In solitude did the heavenly heart unfold to a flowery chalice of almighty love, bent towards the holy countenance of the father, and resting on the happily-expectant bosom of the lovely pensive mother. With divine ardour did the prophetic eye of the blooming child look forth into the days of the future, towards his beloved, the offspring of the race of God, careless for his day's earthly destiny. The most child-like spirits, wondrously seized with a deep, heart-felt love, collected soon around him; as flowers, a new and unknown life budded forth upon his path. Words inexhaustible, the gladdest tidings fell, as sparks from a heavenly spirit, from his friendly lips. From a distant coast, born under Hellas' cheerful sky, a minstrel came to Palestine, and yielded his whole heart to the wondrous child: –

"The youth art thou, who for uncounted time,
    Upon our graves hast stood with hidden meaning;
In hours of darkness a consoling sign,
    Of higher manhood's joyous, hailed beginning;
That which hath made our soul so long to pine,
    Now draws us hence, sweet aspirations winning.
In Death, eternal Life hath been revealed:
And thou art Death, by thee we first are healed."

The minstrel wandered, full of joy, towards Hindostan, the heart elated with the sweetest love, which, beneath yonder heavens, he poured forth in fiery songs, so that a thousand hearts inclined towards him, and with a thousand branches grew towards heaven the joyous tidings. Soon after the minstrel's departure, the precious life became a sacrifice to the deep guilt of man: he died in youthful years, torn from the world he loved, from the weeping mother and lamenting friends. His mouth of love emptied the dark cup of inexpressible affliction. In fearful anguish approached the hour of the new world's birth. Deeply was he touched with the old world's fearful death – the weight of the old world fell heavily upon him. Once more he gazed placidly upon the mother, then came the loosening hand of eternal love, and he slumbered. Few days only hung a deep veil over the swelling sea, over the quaking land; the beloved ones wept countless tears; the mystery was unsealed: the ancient stone heavenly spirits raised from the dark grave. Angels sat beside the slumberer, tenderly formed out of his dreams. Awakened in the new glory of a god, he ascended the height of the new-born world; and with his own hand buried within the deserted sepulchre the old one's corpse, and with almighty hand placed over it the stone no power can raise.

Yet do thy dear ones weep rich tears of joy, tears of emotion, and of eternal gratitude beside thy grave; even yet, with glad alarm, do they behold thee rise, themselves with thee; behold thee weeping, with sweet feeling, on the happy bosom of thy mother, solemnly walking with thy friends, speaking words as if broken from the tree of life; see thee hasten, full of longing, to thy Father's arms, bringing the young race of man, and the cup of a golden future, which shall never be exhausted. The mother soon followed thee in heavenly triumph; she was the first to join thee in the new home. Long ages have flown by since then, and ever in yet higher glory hath thy new creation grown, and thousands from out of pain and misery have, full of faith and longing, followed thee; roam with thee and the heavenly virgin in the realm of love, serve in the temple of heavenly Death, and are in eternity thine.

"Lifted is the stone,
    Manhood hath arisen:
Still are we thine own,
    Unharmed by bond or prison.
When earth – life – fade away
    In the last meal's solemn gladness,
Around thy cup dare stray
No trace of grief or sadness.

To the marriage, Death doth call,
    The brilliant lamps are lighted;
The virgins come, invited,
    And oil is with them all.
Space now to space is telling
    How forth thy train hath gone,
The voice of stars is swelling
With human tongue and tone!

To thee, Maria, hallowed,
    A thousand hearts are sent;
In this dark life and shadowed,
    On thee their thoughts are bent:
The soul's releasement seeing
    They, longing, seek its rest;
By thee pressed, holy being,
Upon thy faithful breast.

How many who, once glowing,
    Earth's bitterness have learned,
Their souls with grief o'erflowing,
    To thee have sadly turned;
Thou pitying hast appearéd,

In many an hour of pain;
We come to thee now, wearied,
There ever to remain.

By no cold grave now weepeth
  A faithful love, forlorn;
Each still love's sweet rights keepeth,
  From none will they be torn.
To soften his sad longing
  Her fires doth Night impart;
From heaven cherubs thronging,
Hold watch upon his heart.

Content, our life advancing
  To a life that shall abide,
Each flame its worth enhancing,
  The soul is glorified.
The starry host shall sink then
  To bright and living wine,
The golden draught we drink then,
And stars ourselves shall shine.

Love released, lives woundless,
  No separation more;
While life swells free and boundless
  As a sea without a shore.
One night of glad elation,
  One joy that cannot die,
And the sun of all creation
Is the face of the Most High."

VI

LONGING FOR DEATH

Below, within the earth's dark breast,
    From realms of light departing,
There sorrow's pang and sigh oppressed
    Is signal of our starting.
In narrow boat we ferry o'er
Speedily to heaven's shore.

To us be hallowed endless Night,
    Hallowed eternal slumber!
The day hath withered us with light,
    And troubles beyond number.
No more 'mong strangers would we roam;
We seek our Father, and our home.

Upon this world, what do we here,
    As faithful, fond, and true men?
The Old but meets with scorn and sneer: –
    What care we for the New, then?
Oh, lone is he, and sadly pines,
Who loves with zeal the olden times!

Those old times when the spirits light
    To heaven as flame ascended;
The Father's hand and features bright
    When men yet comprehended;
When many a mortal, lofty-souled,
Yet bore the mark of heavenly mould.

Those olden times when budded still

The stems of ancient story,
And children, to do Heaven's will,
    In pain and death sought glory;
Those times when life and pleasure spoke,
Yet many a heart with fond love broke.

Those old times when in fires of youth
    Was God himself revealéd,
And early death, in love and truth,
    His sweet existence sealéd,
Who put not from him care and pain,
That dear to us he might remain.

With trembling longing these we see,
    By darkness now belated,
In Time's dominions ne'er will be
    Our ardent thirsting sated.
First to our home 'tis need we go,
Seek we these holy times to know.

And our return what still can stay?
    Long have the best-loved slumbered;
Their grave bounds for us life's drear way,
    Our souls with grief are cumbered.
All that we have to seek is gone,
The heart is full – the world is lone.

Unending, with mysterious flame,
    O'er us sweet awe is creeping;
Methought from viewless distance came
    An echo to our weeping;
The loved ones long for us on high,
And sent us back their pining sigh.

Below, to seek the tender bride,

To Jesus, whom we cherish!
Good cheer! lo, greys the even-tide, –
   Love's agonies shall perish. –
A dream – our fetters melt, at rest
We sink upon the Father's breast.

HYMNS TO THE NIGHT.[2]

Translated by M.J. Hope[3]

2 This is parts 1 to 5, about a third of *Hymns To the Night*.
3 The text is from *Novalis: His Life, Thoughts and Works* edited and translated by M.J. Hope, published by A.C. McClurg, Chicago, 1891.

1

What living, feeling being loves not the gorgeous hues which proclaim the dawn of day? The ever-moving stars, as they whirl in boundless ether, hail the dawn — bright herald of the day; the glistening rocks hail its rays, the tender, growing plants raise their pure eyes rejoicing, and the wild animal joins in the happy chorus which welcomes another day.

More than all these rejoices the glorious Being, the Monarch of the Earth. His deep, thoughtful eyes survey His creation, His melodious voice summons nature to resume her magic works. He binds or looses a million ties, and stamps all earthly life with some impress of His power. His presence reveals the marvels of the Kingdom of Earth. But sacred Night, with her unspoken mysteries, draws me to her. The world is far, far away, buried in a deep and lonely grave. My heart is full of sadness. Let me dissolve in drops of dew, and join the beloved dust. Long past memories, youthful ambitions, childhood's dreams, a long life of brief joys and blighted hopes, pass before me — dusky forms, like evening mist. In another region merry day returns triumphant. Will it never return to us, its children, who await its coming in childlike trust? What stirs this weary heart, and banishes my sorrow? Dost thou feel pity for us, O holy Night?

What soothing influence pervades my being? What hand sheds costly opiate on my throbbing heart? The wings of fancy no longer droop, fresh energy arises within me. In joyful surprise I see a calm, grave face bend lovingly over me, the face of a tender mother, beaming with eternal youth. How poor and childish in comparison are the joys of day. How blessed and consoling the return of night. The active work of day is over, the boundless ocean of space, with its lustrous spheres, proclaims Night's eternal power and presence. The eyes of the Night are countless hosts of glittering orbs, a glory far exceeding that of Day. They see far beyond the most distant of those countless hosts; they need no light to perceive the unfathomable depth of that loving Spirit who fills boundless space with happiness. All hail! Queen of the Earth! thou herald of holier worlds, thou revealer of holy love! Much loved sun of the night, thou art her gift.

My whole being awakes. I am thine, and thou art mine. Night has aroused me to life and manhood. Consume my earthly frame, draw me into deeper and closer union, and may our bridal night endure for ever.

2

Must Day return again? Will earthly influences never cease? Unholy toil desecrates the heavenly calm of Night. When shall the mystic sacrifice of love burn for ever? Light has its own fixed limits, but Night has a boundless unfathomable dominion; the reign of Sleep has no end. Holy Sleep! shed thy blest balm on the hallowed Night of this earthly sphere. Only fools fail to understand Thee, and know of no other sleep than the shades which the actual night casts over us in kindly pity. They see Thee not in the purple blood of the grape, in the golden oil of the almond, in the dusky sap of the poppy. They guess not that it is Thou who hoverest around the tender maiden, making her heart the temple of Heaven; nor dream that it is Thou, heavenly messenger, who bearest the key which opens the dwellings of the Blessed.

3

Once, as I shed bitter tears, all my hope dissolved in pain, as I stood alone by the grave which hid from my sight, in its dark narrow space, the form of my life; lonely as none had ever been, pursued by unspeakable anguish, powerless even to express my grief. I looked around for help. Forward I could not go – nor backward, but clung with unutterable longing to a transient extinguished life. Lo! from the azure distance, down from the heights of my old happiness, came a chill breath of dusk, which severed at once the bonds of birth, the fetters of light. Earthly glory vanished, bearing with it the sorrows of my heart; my sadness had fallen from me into an unknown, unfathomable world. Spirit of Night, heavenly rest, overshadowed me. My enfranchised new-born soul soared over the gently rising scene. The lonely grave turned to a cloud of dust, and through the cloud I discerned the transfigured features of my beloved. Eternity shone in her eyes, I clasped her hand, my tears formed a brilliant indissoluble chain. Eons of ages fled into space like scattered clouds. On her neck I wept the rapturous tears of the new life – it was my first, my only dream; and ever since I feel this changeless, everlasting faith in the heaven of Night and its light – my beloved.

4

I know when the last day shall come – when Light no longer shall be scared by Night and Love: then slumber shall not cease, and existence shall become an endless dream. Heavenly weariness oppresses me – long and dreamy was my pilgrimage to the Holy Grave, crushing was the cross I bore. He who has drunk of the crystal wave, which wells forth from the gloomy grave, on which earth's billows break, he who has stood on earth's border-land, and perceived that new country, the dwelling of Night, returns not to the tumult of life, to the land where light reigns amid ceaseless unrest. He builds himself a refuge far from the tumult – a peaceful home, and awaits the welcome hour, when he, too, shall be drawn into the crystal wave. All that savours of earth floats on the surface, and is driven back by tempests, but what love has hallowed flows in hidden channels, to another region where it mingles – a fragrant essence – with those loved ones who have fallen asleep.

Ah! merry Light, thou still arousest the weary to their task, and strivest to inspire me, too, with cheerful life; but thou hast no charm to tempt me from my cherished memories. With joy I watch the busy hands, and look around to fulfil my own duty, I praise thy glorious works, admire the matchless blending of thy cunning designs, watch the varied workings of the busy hours, and seek to discover the symmetry and laws which rule the marvels of endless space and measureless ages. But my heart remains ever true to Night and her daughter, creative Love. Canst thou show me one ever-faithful heart? Has thy sun a friendly glance for me? Do thy stars hold out a welcoming hand?

Do they return the gentle pressure and the caressing word? Hast thou clothed them in colour and beauty?' What joys or pleasure can life offer to outweigh the chain of death. Does not all that inspires us bear the colours of Night? Night bears thee gently like a mother; to her thou owest all thy glory. Thou wouldest have sunk into endless space, had not Night upheld thee, and bound thee, till earth arose. Truly existed long ere thou wert: I and my sisters were sent to dwell in thy world, and hallow it with love, to make it an enduring memorial; to plant it with unfading flowers. Not yet have these blossoms opened, few are the traces which mark our way. But the end of time is at hand; then thou wilt rejoin us, and gently fade away, full of longing and fervent desire. All thy busy restlessness will end in heavenly freedom, a blessed home-coming. With bitter grief I acknowledge thy forsaking of our home, thine unconquered hatred to the old glorious heaven.

But in vain is Thy wrath and fury. The Cross stands firm for ever, the banner of our race.

5

The many scattered races of mankind lay bound for ages in the grasp of an iron fate. Light was hidden from their weary souls. The eternal world was the home and dwelling of the Gods. Its mysterious form had existed from eternity. Over the glowing mountains of the East abode the Sun, with its all-pervading heat and light. An aged Giant bore the Earth on his shoulders. The Titans, the first children of Mother Earth — who had waged impious war against the new glorious race of Gods and their kinsfolk, the merry race of men — lay fast bound under the mountains. The dark green depths of Ocean was the lap of a Goddess. A gay, luxurious race dwelt in the crystal grottoes. Beasts, trees, flowers, and animals had the gift of speech. Richer was the flavour of the grapes, for a God dwelt in the luxuriant vine; the golden sheaves took their birth from a loving motherly Goddess; and love was the sweet service rendered to the deities. Age followed age — a ceaseless spring, and the happy life of Earth's children was ever enlivened by celestial presences. All races honoured the flashing, many-hued flame, as the highest manifestation in life. Only one shadow obscured the common joy — the cruel spectre of Death. This mysterious decree — separation from all that was loved and lovely — weighed heavy on the hearts of all; even the Gods could find no remedy for this evil. Unable to overcome the menacing fate, man strove to cast a glamour of beauty over the ghastly phantom, and pictured him as a lovely youth extinguishing a torch, and sinking to rest. Still the cruel enigma remained unsolved, and spoke of the irresistible might of some unknown power. The old world waned; the flowers of the first Paradise faded away; and the race of men, casting off their early innocence, strayed into a wild, uncultivated desert. The Gods and their retinues vanished from Earth. Nature stood lonely and lifeless, bound in the iron chains of custom and laws. The bloom was brushed from life. Faith took flight from the dreary scene; and with her fled her heavenly companion Fancy, who could cast over all things her magic vesture. A cruel North wind swept over the barren waste, and the devastated wonder-home was blown into space. Heaven's blue ocean showed new dazzling spheres, and the Spirit of the World withdrew to higher regions to await the dawn of a renewed earth. Light ceased to be the abode and the symbol of the Gods; they covered themselves with the veil of Night. Night was the cradle of the coming age; in it the Gods took refuge, and sleep came upon them, until a new era should call them forth in new and more glorious forms. The new era arose at last amidst a nation scorned and despised, a people who had cast off their native innocence. In poverty was born the Son of the first Virgin Mother, mysterious offspring of heavenly origin. The wise sons of the East were first to acknowledge the commencement of the strange, new epoch, and humbly bent their way to worship the King in His lowly cradle – a mystic star guided their wandering steps. They did Him homage, offering Him the sweetness and brightness of the earth, the gold and the perfume, both miracles of nature. The Heavenly Heart unfolded slowly – a flower chalice of Almighty love, with eyes upturned to a Divine Father, while His head rested on the tender bosom of a loving earthly mother. With prophetic eye and godlike zeal, the blooming Child, despising the cruel days of earthly conflict before Him, looked far ahead to the future of His beloved face, the offshoots of a divine root. Soon He gathered around Him a loving band of childlike hearts. A strange, new life arose, like that of the flowers of the field; unceasing words of wisdom and utterances of deepest love fell from His lips, like sparks of divine fire. From the far shores of Hellas, and her sunny skies, the poet came to Palestine, and laid his heart at the feet of the Wonder-Child.

Oh! Thou art He who from unending years
Hast looked with pity on our earthly tomb;
Thou gav'st a sign of life in deepest night,
And Thou wilt bring our higher manhood home.
Thou hast upheld us here mid grief and tears.
Lead Thou our nobler longings up to Heaven;

In death alone eternal life is found.
For Thou art death, and Thou our life hast given.

Full of joy, his heart beating with new love and hope, the singer
bent his way to Hindustan, pouring out under its cloudless sky such
burning songs, that myriads of hearts turned to him, and the joyful
news spread far and near. Soon after the poet left, the precious Life
fell a sacrifice to fallen man: He died young, torn away from the
much-loved earth, His weeping mother, and His faint-hearted friends.
The moment of anguish, the birth of the new world was at hand. He
fought with the old dreaded form of death; struggled hard to shake
off the clutch of the old world; His sweet lips drained the bitter
chalice of unspeakable anguish. Once more He cast a loving glance
at His mother, then came the delivering hand of Mighty Love, and He
fell asleep. For many days a thick mist lay on the raging waters and
the quaking earth: countless were the tears shed by those who loved
Him: the secret of the grave was made clear, and heavenly spirits
rolled away the heavy stone from the tomb. Angels watched by the
slumbering Form: rising in new godlike glory, He soared to the
heights of the newly-made world, buried the old earthly shape in the
depths of a cavern, and laid His mighty hand on it, so that no power
might ever move it.

The loving ones still wept by His grave, but they wept tears of
emotion and gratitude. Again they see Thee and rejoice at Thy
resurrection: they see Thee weeping on Thy mother's sacred bosom:
they walk once more as friends, listening to words like leaves
fluttering from the Tree of Life: they behold Thee hasten with untold
longing to the Father's arms, bearing aloft the new manhood and the
victorious chalice. The mother soon hastened to join Thy triumph:
she was the first to enter the New Home. Long years have passed
since *then* and Thy new creation soars to higher powers: thousands
and thousands drawn by Thee from bitter grief and pain now roam
with Thee and the heavenly Virgin in the Kingdom of Love, serve in
the Temple of Divine Death, and are Thine eternally.

HYMNS TO THE NIGHT

Translated by Paul B. Thomas[4]

---
4 From *The German Classics: Masterpieces of German Literature* ed. Kuno Francke,
1914. This is Parrt 1 only.

1

Who, that hath life and the gift of perception, loves not more than all the marvels seen far and wide in the space about him Light, the all-gladdening, with its colors, with its beams and its waves, its mild omnipresence as the arousing day? The giant world of restless stars breathes it, as were it the innermost soul of life, and lightly floats in its azure flood; the stone breathes it, sparkling and ever at rest, and the dreamy, drinking plant, and the savage, ardent, manifold fashioned beast; but above all the glorious stranger with the thoughtful eyes, the airy step, and the lightly-closed, melodious lips. Like a king of terrestrial nature it calls every power to countless transformations, it forms and dissolves innumerable alliances and surrounds every earthly creature with its heavenly effulgence. Its presence alone reveals the marvelous splendor of the realms of the world.

Downward I turn my eyes to Night, the holy, ineffable, mysterious. Far below lies the world, sunk in a deep vault; void and lonely is its place. Deep melancholy is wafted through the chords of the breast. In drops of dew I'd fain sink down and mingle with the ashes. Far-off memories, desires of youth, dreams of childhood, long life's brief joys and vain hopes appear in gray garments like the evening mist after sunset. Light has pitched its gay tents in other regions. Will it perchance never return to its children, who are waiting for it with the faith of innocence?

What is it that suddenly wells up so forebodingly from beneath the heart and smothers the gentle breath of melancholy? Dark Night, dost thou also take pleasure in us? What hast thou beneath thy mantle which touches my soul with invisible force? Precious balsam drops from the bunch of poppies in thy hand. Thou raisest up the heavy wings of the soul; vaguely and inexpressibly we feel ourselves moved. Joyously fearful, I see an earnest face, which gently and reverently bends over me, and amid endlessly entangled locks shows the sweet youth of the mother. How poor and childish does Light seem to me now! How joyful and blessed the departure of day! Only for that reason, then, because Night turns thy servants from thee, didst thou scatter in the wide expanse of space the shining stars, to make known thine omnipotence and thy return, during the periods of thine absence? More heavenly than those twinkling stars seem to us the everlasting eyes which Night has opened within us. Farther they see than the palest of those numberless hosts; not needing light, they fathom the depths of a loving heart, filling a higher space with unspeakable delight.

Praise be to the queen of the world, to the high harbinger of holy worlds, to the fostress of blissful love! She sends thee to me, gentle sweetheart, lovely sun of the night. Now I am awake, for I am thine and mine; thou hast proclaimed to me that night is life and made a man of me. Consume my body with spiritual fire, that I may ethereally blend with thee, and then the bridal night may last forever.

TRANSCENDENT POETRY:
A NOTE ON NOVALIS

The world must be romanticized.

Novalis, *Pollen and Fragments* (56)

Poetry is what is truly and absolutely real, this is the kernel of my philosophy. The more poetic, the more true.

Novalis[1]

Novalis is the most mystical of the German Romantic poets. He is at once the most typical and the most unusual of the German Romantic poets – indeed, of all Romantic poets.[2] He is supremely idealistic, far more so than Johann Wolfgang von Goethe or Heinrich Heine. He died young, which makes him, like Percy Bysshe Shelley and John Keats, something of a hero (or martyr). He did not write as much as Shelley,

1 Novalis: *Works* (Minor), III, 11
2 See Richard Faber, 1970; Heinz Ritter: "Die geistlichen Lieder des Novalis. Ihre Datierung und Entstehung", *Jahrbuch der deutschen Schiller–Gesellschaft* IV, 1960, 308–42; Friedrich Hiebel: *Novalis*, Francke, Bern 1972; Curt Grutzmacher, 1964; Géza von Molnár, 1970; John Neubauer, 1972; Bruce Haywood, 1959.

but his work, like that of Keats or Arthur Rimbaud, promised much. For Michael Hamburger, Novalis' work is almost totally idealistic: 'Novalis's philosophy, then, is not mystical, but utopian. That is why his imaginative works are almost wholly lacking in conflict. They are a perpetual idyll'.[3] It's true, Novalis' work is supremely idealistic, and utopian. But it is also mystical, because it points towards the invisible, unseen, unknown, and aims to reach that ecstatic realm. He wrote:

> The sense of poetry has much in common with that for mysticism. It is the sense of the peculiar, personal, unknown, mysterious, for what is to be *revealed*, the necessary-accidental. It represents the unrepresentable. It sees the invisible, feels the unfeelable, etc... The sense for poetry has a close relationship with the sense for augury and the religious sense, with the sense for prophecy in general.[4]

Novalis was born Georg Philipp Friedrich von Hardenberg on May 2, 1772 in Oberwiederstedt. He studied law between 1790 and 1794 at Jena, Wittenberg and Leipzig. There he met many of the leading literary lights, such as Johann Wolfgang von Goethe, Johann Gottfried Herder, Jean Paul (Johann Paul Friedrich Richter), the Schlegels, Ludwig von Tieck and Friedrich Wilhelm Joseph Schelling. Later, in 1797, Novalis studied at the Mining Academy in Freiburg. He began publishing in 1798. His chief works include: *Faith and Love or the King and the Queen, Pollen, The Novices at Sais, Heinrich von Ofterdingen, Christendom or Europa* and *Hymns To the Night.*[5] He was engaged to Sophie von Kühn from 1794-97, and to Julie von Charpentier from 1798 to his death in 1801. He died on March 25, 1801 in Weißenfels, from tuberculosis.

Novalis was passionately in love with his beloved, Sophie, whom he had met in October, 1794, when she was twelve. They were engaged in

---

3 M. Hamburger: *Reason and Energy*, 97
4 Novalis: *Novalis Schriften,* 3, 686
5 The translator of this edition of *Hymns To the Night,* George MacDonald (1824-95), was influenced by Novalis. MacDonald's works included *Phantastes* (1858), *Lilith* (1895), *Bannerman's Boyhood* and the *Curdie* children's stories: *The Princess and the Goblin*(1872) and *The Princess and Curdie*(1882). Lewis Carroll and John Ruskin were among MacDonald's literary friends. The Scottish fantasist was a significant influence on J.R.R. Tolkien and C.S. Lewis, among others.

March, 1795 (Sophie was 13; Novalis was 22). Novalis was devastated when she died on March 19, 1797, two days after her fifteenth birthday, and by the death of his brother Erasmus less than a month later. 'My main task should be', he wrote, 'to bring everything into a relationship to [Sophia's] idea.'6

After the death of Sophia von Kühn, Novalis wrote to Karl Wilhelm Friedrich Schlegel from Tennstedt, near Grüningen, where she was buried:

> You can imagine how I feel in this neighbourhood, the old witness of my and her glory. I still feel a secret enjoyment to be so close to her grave. It attracts me ever more closely, and this now occasionally constitutes my indescribable happiness. My autumn has come, and I feel so free, usually so vigorous – something can come of me after all. This much I solemnly assure you as become absolutely clear to me what a heavenly accident her death has been – the key to everything – a marvellously appropriate event. Only through it could various things be absolutely resolved and much immaturity overcome. A simple mighty force has come to reflection within me. My love has become a flame gradually consuming everything earthly.7

Sophie von Kühn was for Novalis something like Dante Alighieri's Beatrice Portinari or Francesco Petrarch's Laura de Noyes, or Maurice Scève's Délie; that is, a soul–image or *anima* figure, someone pure and holy. Further, Sophie the person fused for Novalis with 'Sophia' of Gnostic philosophy, the Goddess about whom C.G. Jung has written so eloquently.

> My favourite study [wrote Novalis in 1796] has the same name as my fiancée. Sophie is her name – philosophy is the soul of my life and the key to my innermost self. Since that acquaintance, I also have become completely amalgamated with that study.8

Sophia is the Goddess of Wisdom; she is an incarnation for poets and mystics of the Black Goddess, a deity who presides over the unknown, the dark things, occultism and witchcraft. Novalis was very interested in the occult, in magic and hermeticism, in Neoplatonism, alchemy,

6 Novalis: ib, 4, 37
7 Novalis, in, 4, 220
8 Novalis, letter to Friedrich Schlegel, 8 July 1796, in *Novalis Schriften,* op.cit., 4, 188

theosophy, the *Qabbalah*, and other belief systems. Novalis was fascinated by the invisible realm, the things that are unseen but he knows are there, which is the realm of occultism. As he writes: 'We are bound nearer to the unseen than to the visible.'[9]

Apart from his small collection of lyrics, and his *Hymnen an die Nacht*, one of Novalis' major works was his (unfinished) *Blütenstaub (Pollen)* and *Glauben und Liebe (Faith and Love)*, collections of philosophical fragments. These together form an æsthetics of religion, and a mysticism of poetry.

❦

Some notes on German Romanticism are worth making here: the world of German Romantic poetry holds many of the same tenets as that of British and French Romanticism. The term 'Romanticism' means for me here a lyrical, emotional, religious and self-conscious form of art which can be applied to many modern artists, as well as the Romantics themselves.[10]

One of the key elements of Romantic poetry, of German Romantic poetry especially, and of all poetry generally, is the concept of unity. For the poet, all things are connected together.

> In our mind [wrote Novalis], everything is connected in the most peculiar, pleasant, and lively manner. The strangest things come together by virtue of one space, one time, an odd similarity, an error, some accident. In this manner, curious unities and peculiar connections originate – one thing reminds us of everything, becomes the sign of many things. Reason and imagination are united through time and space in the most extraordinary manner, and we can say that each thought, each phenomenon of our mind is the most individual part of an altogether individual totality.[11]

9 Novalis: *Pollen*, 125.
10 On Romanticism, see Jürgen Habermas: *The Philosophical Discourse of Modernity*, tr. Frederick Lawrence, MIT Press, Cambridge Mass., 1987. On German Romanticism, see David Simpson *et al*, eds: *German Aesthetic and Literary Criticism*, Cambridge University Press, 3 vols, 1984–5; H.G. Schenk: *The Mind of the European Romantics*, Constable, 1966; M.H. Abrams: *Natural Supernaturalism: Tradition and Revolution in Romantic Literature*, Norton, New York, 1971; Marshall Brown, 1979; Philippe Lacoue–Labarthe & Jean-Luc Nancy, eds, 1988; Azade Seyhan: *Representation and its Discontents: The Critical Legacy of German Romanticism*, University of California Press, Berkeley, 1992.
11 Novalis, *Novalis Schriften*, 3, 650-1.

What connects everything is the poet's sensibility, awareness, imagination, talents, feelings, call them what you will. Poetry is very much like Western magic in this respect. Magicians speak of the cardinal rule of hermeticism and magicke as being the hermetic tenet of the Emerald Table of Hermes Trismegistus: *as above, so below* This dictum applies to poetry as much to magic. Basically, the view is that all things are one even as they are separate/ different/ scattered everywhere. Sufi mystics speak of 'unity in multiplicity' and 'multiplicity in unity', the 'unity' for them being Allah. For poets and magicians, founded in the Western Neoplatonic, Renaissance, humanist, magical tradition, 'the One' is only occasionally identified with God.

For (the Romantic) poets, the *as above, so below* worldview means that inner and outer are identical, that what happens inside, psychologically, is mirrored and influences the outer, physical world. The two worlds interconnect and influence each other. As Novalis writes: 'What is outside me, is really within me, is mind – and vice versa'.[12] Further, the world is a continuum for the poet, so that colours are associated with particular planets, say, or angels, or flowers, or metals. This view of the oneness of all things occurs not only in Romantic poetry, but in most of poetry, from Sappho in the ancient world onwards. It is, partly, the basis for the 'pathetic fallacy', the ubiquitous poetic metaphor, where Sappho can say that erotic desire is like a wind shaking oak trees on a mountainside.

The Romantic philosophy of unity develops into Charles Baudelaire's 'theory of correspondences', which was later taken up by Arthur Rimbaud, Stéphane Mallarmé and Paul Valéry. Friedrich Schlegel, one of the major theorists of Romantic poetry, speaks of Romantic art as unifying poetry and philosophy, which is one of the hallmarks of Romantic poetry, German or otherwise. 'Romantic poetry is a progressive universal poetry', wrote Schlegel.[13] He argued for a new mythology of poetry, a universal mythopœia, which would connect all things together, a 'hieroglyphic expression of nature around us'.[14]

12 Novalis, *Novalis Schriften,* 3, 429
13 F. Schlegel: *Kritische Friedrich Schlegel Ausgabe,* Schöningh, Paderborn, 1958, II, 182
14 F. Schlegel, in ib., II, 318

Folklore and fairy tales are another element: much of German Romanticism uses all kinds of folklore – the Grimms, for instance, with their very influential collection, *Children's and Household Tales,* and their collecting (and rewriting) of fairy tales. Ludwig von Tieck's works contain much fantastic material, and he uses fairy tales in his fictions, including Charles Perrault's *Puss in Boots* fairy tale in his *Der gestiefelte Kater*[15] A.W. Schlegel wrote: 'Myth, like language, generally, a necessary product of the human poetic power, an arche-poetry of humanity'.[16]

Novalis wrote of fairy tales: 'All fairy tales are dreams of that home-like world that is everywhere and nowhere.'[17] Figures such as Isolde and Tristan, Tannhäuser, of Arthurian legend, appear in German Romantic poetry. Romanticism also employs all manner of hermetic or occult thought, from Gnosticism (in Novalis's philosophy), Qabbalism, Rosicrucianism, alchemy, magic, astronomy, etc (in Franz Brentano's *Die Romanzen vom Rosenkrantz* alchemy in Johann Wolfgang von Goethe's *Faust,* etc).

The Hellenism of German Romanticism ties in with (and is inextricable from) the paganism of Romanticism. The German Romantics, like their British counterparts, exalted pagan beliefs, though theirs was a stylized, self-conscious form of paganism, which took up certain beliefs or rites and ignored others. Heinrich Heine wrote that the first Romantics

> acted out of a pantheistic impulse of which they themselves were not aware. The feeling which they believed to be a nostalgia for the Catholic Mother Church was of deeper origin than they guessed, and their reverence and preference for the heritage of the Middle Ages, for the popular beliefs, diabolism, magical practices, and witchcraft of that era… all this was a suddenly reawakened but unrecognized leaning toward the pantheism of the ancient

---

15 See Rolf Stamm: *Ludwig Tieck's späte Novellen,* Kohlhamer, Stuttgart, 1973; Raimund Belgardt: "Poetic Imagination and External Reality in Tieck", *Essays in German Literature Festschrift,* ed. Michael S. Batts, University of British Columbia Press, 1968, 41-61; Rosemarie Helge: *Motive und Motivstrukturen bei Ludwig Tieck,* Kummerle, Göppingen, 1974
16 A.W. Schlegel: *Kritische Ausgabe der Verlesungen,* ed. Ernst Behler & Frank Jolles, Schöningen, Paderborn, 1989-, I, 49
17 Novalis, *Novalis Schriften,* 2. 564

Germans.[18]

The paganism of Romanticism is a part of pantheism, as in the Classicism of painters such as Nicolas Poussin and Claude Lorrain, or nature worship. Heinrich Heine called pantheism 'the secret religion of Germany'.[19]

The Romantics, including Novalis, exalted nature (German Romanticism had its 'Naturphilosophie', a non-scientific notion stemming partly from the work of Friedrich Wilhelm Joseph Schelling and Georg Wilhelm Friedrich Hegel). But, again, nature is mediated through the highly self-conscious and heavily stylized mechanisms of poetry. Images of nature abound in most forms of Romantic poetry. Nature is the backdrop to their poetic out-pourings, but it is always nature seen from the vantage point of culture.[20]

German Romantic poetry, like all Romantic poetry (like all poetry, one might say), has idealistic and utopian elements. German Romantic poetry, in particular, is marked by a vivacious, sometimes over-developed idealism (and utopianism), which comes as much from the philosopher Plato as from Immanuel Kant. 'Transcendental idealism' is a term often applied to German Romantic poetics. 'I call transcendental all knowledge which is not so much occupied with objects as with the mode of our cognition of objects', remarked Kant in the *Critique of Pure Reason*,[21] underlining the subjectivity (as with René Descartes) that is at the centre of post-Renaissance philosophy. There is a philosophy, Johann Gottlieb Fichte argued, that is beyond being and beyond consciousness, a philosophy that aims for 'the absolute unity between their separateness.'[22]

※

Novalis, like the other (German) Romantics, believed in the magical/ religious unity of the world. For him, all things were united, in one way

18 H. Heine: *Salon II*, 1852, 250-1
19 H. Heine: *Works*, 3, 571
20 Novalis has a fascinating view of nature as the mother, a refuge: 'the reason why people are so attached to Nature is probably that, being spoilt children, they are afraid of the father and take refuge with the mother'.
21 Immanuel Kant: *Werke*, de Gruyter, Berlin, 1968, III, 43
22 J. Fichte, letter, 23 June 1804, quoted in E. Behler, 19

or another. Novalis was one of the first artists to bring together many seemingly diverse practices and philosophies. Leonardo da Vinci had drawn together botany, biology, anatomy, natural science, engineering, mathematics and other strands of thought in his Renaissance art, and Novalis did the same. The metaphysical synthesis was called *Totalwissenschaft*, a total knowledge.

Novalis learnt much from Friedrich Schlegel, during his time at Jena, one of the centres of German Romanticism. Schlegel wrote at length of the unifying spirit of art, where poetry and philosophy merge: the aim of Romantic poetry, Schlegel asserted, was not only 'to unite all the separate species of poetry and put poetry in touch with philosophy and rhetoric', but also to

> use poetry and prose, inspiration and criticism, the poetry of art and the poetry of nature; and make poetry lively and sociable, and life and society poetic; poeticize wit and fill and saturate the forms of art with every kind of good, solid matters for instruction, and animate them with the pulsation of humour.[23]

Novalis' philosophy may be called 'transcendent philosophy', as his poetry might be called 'transcendent poetry'. He called it 'magisch', 'Magie', his 'magic idealism'.[24] It is a mixture of poetry and philosophy, a poetry of philosophy and a philosophy of poetry.[25] 'Transcendental poetry is an admixture of poetry and philosophy,'[26] he writes. And again: 'Poetry is the champion of philosophy... Philosophy is the theory of poetry.' (ib., 56) Poetry becomes philosophy, and philosophy becomes poetry. Or as he put it: 'Die Welt wird Traum, der Traum wird Welt' ('World becomes dream, dream becomes world'). Friedrich Schlegel wrote in the *Athenæum* (fragment 451): 'Universality can attain harmony only through the conjunction of poetry and philosophy'.[27]

23 F. Schlegel, *Gespräch über die Poesie, Kritische Friedrich Schlegel Ausgabe* Schöningh, Paderborn, 1958, 182
24 Novalis: *Works* (Minor), Paris, 1837, III
25 See Manfred Frank: "Die Philosophie des sogenannten "magischen Idealismus"", *Euph*, LXIII, 1969, 88–116; Karl Heinz Volkmann–Schluck, 1967, 45–53; Theodor Haering, 1954; G. Hughes, 66; Manfred Dick, 1967, 223–77; Hugo Kuhn: *Text und Theorie*, Metzler, Stuttgart 1967
26 Novalis: *Pollen and Fragments*, 57
27 F. Schlegel, *Lucinde and the Fragments*, tr. Peter Firchow, University of Minnesota Press, Minneapolis 1971, 240

Kept by Novalis as a collection of fragments, *Pollen* has affinities with the maxims of Friedrich Nietzsche, the thoughts in Blaise Pascal's *Pensées,* with Jacob Boehme's writings and other mystical collections. It is worth quoting from some of these fragments, which show Novalis at his most idealistic and pithy. His statements summarize the (German) Romantic position on poetry, and the basics of all poetics. First of all, he muses on interiority:

> Toward the Interior goes the arcane way. In us, or nowhere, is the Eternal with its worlds, the past and future... The seat of the world is there, where the inner world and the outer world touch... The inner world is almost more mine than the outer. It is so heartfelt, so private – man is given fullness in that life – it is so native.[28]

Here Novalis heads straight for one of the prime realms of mysticism: the inner world, the life of the spirit, the imagination, the soul. His distinction, and then fusion, of inner and outer is the beginnings of modern psychology. It is also one of the key aspects of poetry. For the poet, the inner, psychic or spiritual world is as real and as important, and nourishing, as the outer, public world. The two in fact are part of a continuum, both flowing into each other, like the *yin–yang* dualism of Chinese mysticism. The one informs the other in art. They are not separated, that is the key point. They form a unity. As Novalis wrote in his poem 'Know Yourself' (the title comes from the basic tenet of Greek hermeticism): 'There is only one'.[29]

In magic and hermeticism, the fundamental tenet is 'as above, so below', which, in the modern era, becomes the psychological 'as outside, so inside'. Poets have long known about this inside–outside pairing. In William Shakespeare's plays, the external setting of a scene – the opening of *Macbeth,* for instance – indicates the characters' inner feelings. Further, in Shakespeare's Elizabethan theatre, there were few props, and little scenery on stage, so the words became full of images, painting pictures in the audience's mind. Hence, in a different way, inner and outer became fused.

For Novalis, rightly, the seat of the soul is precisely that poetic

---

28 Novalis: *Pollen and Fragments* , 50-53
29 Novalis: *Pollen,* 137

space where 'the inner world and the outer world touch' (150). It was Rainer Maria Rilke who fully developed this inner–outer unity in his lyrics. Rilke is, as we have said, the poet most like Novalis in German poetry. Rilke had his notion of the Angel (in the *Duino Elegies*). The Rilkean Angel is essentially a shaman, and Novalis also speaks at length in his collections of fragments of the poet as shaman. He does not use the term 'shaman', but his 'sorcerer' or 'genius' or 'prophet' is basically the archaic shaman, the angelic traveller to other worlds, the vatic mouthpiece of his/ her cult, the dancing, drumming, musical figure, like Dionysius or Orpheus, who knows how to fly, who can climb the World Tree, who can penetrate the invisible.[30] Novalis writes:

> The sorcerer is a poet. The prophet is to the sorcerer as the man of taste is to the poet... The genuine poet is all–knowing... (50–1)

As Weston La Barre notes in *The Ghost Dance*, there is not much difference between the artist, the genius, the criminal, the psychotic and the mad person. Novalis notes:

> Madness and magic have many similarities. A magician is an artist of madnesses. (79)

Similarly, William Shakespeare wrote in *A Midsummer Night's Dream*: 'The lunatic, the lover and the poet,/ Are of imagination all compact.' (V.i.7) In Shakespeare's art, there are deep connections between lovers, lunatics, poets – and fools. They are all caught up with some kind of 'madness', some kind of 'abnormal', 'extraordinary' subjectivity. Their goals may be different, but they are all connected psychologically. Similarly, for Novalis, as for so many poets, love can be seen as a madness, and there is a narrow dividing line between the religious maniac and the fool. There is the 'holy fool' figure in Russian history, the 'trickster god' in ancient mythology, and King Lear's clown, the court jester who is allowed to transgress the boundaries that others are not allowed to cross.

30 See Mircea Eliade, *Myths, Dreams and Mysteries*, Harper & Row, New York, 1975; *Shamanism: Archaic Techniques of Ecstasy* Princeton University Press, New Jersey, 1972; Weston La Barre: *The Ghost Dance*, Allen & Unwin 1972

Novalis as a poet sees the unity of all things, so he writes: 'All barriers are only there for the traversing' (87). This is the Romantic poet talking here: this is a very Romantic notion, it seems, this perception that barriers are there to be transgressed. This is the poet as social rebel speaking, knowing that art must go to extremes. Thus, madness, poetry, idiocy, genius and love form a continuum which is life itself.

In Novalis's *œuvre*, love and mysticism, the secular and the sacred, art and religion, fuse. Thus, in Novalis' 'magic idealism', we hear of the mysticism of love, or the religious nature of art. In this he is no different from other Romantics, such as William Wordsworth or Victor Hugo. For Novalis, life itself is sacred. 'Our whole life is a divine service', he writes (124). In this Novalis is in accord with writers such as D.H. Lawrence, who regarded life itself as holy, or the artist and sculptor Eric Gill, or the cult of the Australian aborigines.

The religion of the aborigines is the 'eternal dreamtime', the mythic, timeless state. For them, life was sacred, and life was sacralized by rituals that include singing. The Australian Bushmen speak of 'singing the world into life'. Rainer Maria Rilke wrote in his *Sonnets For Orpheus*: 'song is existence.' The figure of Orpheus, the mythological poet–as–shaman, features prominently, though he is sometimes hidden, in the works of poets such as Novalis (in his story *Heinrich von Ofterdingen*), Rilke and Arthur Rimbaud. Orpheus' song is his art, and his *raison d'être*. Novalis also wrote of music, and its relation to poetry and religion. The notion of the 'music of the spheres', the celestial harmonies that drive the cosmos, is central to Western religion. For Dante Alighieri, God was at the centre of the concentric circles or wheels of the universe. He was at the heart of the *Rosa Mystica*. For Novalis, the 'One' of Neoplatonism now has many names. In Hinduism it is Brahma; in Taoism it is the Tao; in Zen Buddhism it is Pure Reality; in Tibetan mysticism it is the Clear Light of the Void; and in Islam it is Allah.

Simply being alive, as Mircea Eliade notes, was a sacred act:

In the most archaic phases of culture, *to live as a human being* was in itself *a religious act,* since eating, sexual activity, and labour all had a sacramental value. Experience of the sacred is inherent in man's mode of being in the world. [31]

D.H. Lawrence wrote extensively of 'being alive', about real 'living-ness'. In *Etruscan Places* he defined it in a way of which Novalis would surely approve:

> To the Etruscan all was alive... They [the Etruscans] felt the symbols and danced the sacred dances. For they were always in touch, physically, with the mysteries. [32]

Novalis speaks often of 'mysteries' too. For the occult, hermetic, Neoplatonic, religious artist, there must always be some 'mystery' behind everything. No matter how far you go, there must always be something mysterious behind it. It was true for the participants in the ancient Eleusian Mysteries, and it is the same for Romantic poets. The world is not a machine, nor is it limited. It must be infinite, for, behind everything, there is yet more mystery. There are no limits, yet it is the poet's task to find the limits, and to explore the boundaries.

Novalis looked back to early Christianity, to Neoplatonism and to Greek religion. Like most Romantics, Novalis was very nostalgic. But he might have looked back also to many Hindu sects, to Tantric cults, to Sufi mystics and poets, to Australian aborigines, to the shamans of Siberia and North America, to the Chinese Taoists (Chuang–tzu, Lao–tzu), or to the Confucians (Confucius, Mencius), or to the Zen Buddhist masters (Hui–Neng, Dogen, Jakuin), or to the Ancient Greeks of Epicurus, Heraclitus or Empodecles' day.

What is the purpose of Novalis' cult of 'transcendent poetry'? More life, basically. This was Rainer Maria Rilke's great goal, his Holy Grail: life and more life, more and more of life. That is our goal, Rilke claimed. Poetry is a way of enabling us to be more alive, say Novalis and Rilke:

> Poetry is the great art of constructing transcendental health... Poetry is

31 Mircea Eliade, *Ordeal by Labyrinth,* University of Chicago Press 1984, 154
32 D.H. Lawrence: *Mornings in Mexico and Etruscan Places,* Penguin 1960, 147–9

generation. All compositions must be living individuals. (*Pollen*, 50)

Rainer Maria Rilke says similar things about poetry. In a letter to his Polish translator, Witold von Hulewicz, of November 13, 1925, Rilke explained his notion of the angel: a being that shows us how to be painfully but blissfully alive, living in the transcendent realm of 'the Open', as Rilke called that special poetic place. We must be

> Transformed? Yes, for our task is to stamp this provisional, perishing earth into ourselves so deeply, so painfully and passionately, that its being may rise again, "invisibly", in us.[33]

All you have to do in life is to be. Be what, exactly? Just *be*, says Rainer Maria Rilke: 'all we basically have to do is to *be*, but simply, earnestly, the way the earth simply is', he wrote in *Letters on Cézanne*[34] To simply *be* is really difficult, as Novalis and Rilke admit. Yet it is the goal. To realize, as the Hindu mystics put it, that Thou Art That (*tat tvam asi*). As Novalis commented:

> Art of becoming all–powerful. Art of realizing our intentions totally. (118)

Total fulfilment – it's a tall order, perhaps, but only this ontological totality will do for Novalis. He is supremely idealistic while at the same being totally honest, and totally simple, and totally ordinary. He is optimistic, it seems, when he writes:

> All is seed. (73)

Yet he is also being quite realistic, knowing, as an artist does, that *anything* can be used in art. A transcendent, total art can include *everything.* Nothing is exempt from art, not even nothingness itself. Indeed, nothingness is a large element of some art (Samuel Beckett's compressed texts, for instance, or Ad Reinhardt's black–on–black paintings), as it is a key component in Buddhism and Taoism.

Novalis' idealistic philosophy is all–inclusive. 'All is seed', he writes.

33 Rilke: *Duino Elegies*, tr. J.B. Leishman & Stephen Spender, Hogarth Press, 1957, 157

34 Rilke: *Letters on Cézanne* ed. Clara Rilke, Cape, 1988

All. Or, again, in a different fashion:

All must become nourishment. (65)

Or, again, in a different way, he says:

All can become experiment – all can become an organ. (88)

Meister Eckhart, the German mediæval mystic whose mystical philosophy is in tune with Rainer Maria Rilke's and Novalis' philosophies, wrote:

The seed of God is in us... The seed of a pear tree grows into a pear tree, a hazel seed into a hazel tree, a seed of God into God.[35]

Much of alchemy, hermeticism, witchcraft, Qabbalism and Neoplatonism is concerned with healing, nourishment and rebirth. It was one of Novalis' chief concerns. The philosophical fragments state the basic view of nourishment in a variety of ways. The fragments are deeply poetic. Although they are written in prose, they are clearly poetry. One of Novalis' most powerful sentences is:

Everything can become magical work. (73)

This statement is itself magical. For Novalis, art is for the enrichment of life. Whatever art may do, Novalis says, it must enrich us. 'To enliven all is the aim of life', he asserts (64).

Love features prominently in Novalis' philosophy of poetry and poetry of philosophy. Love – and sex. For, under Novalis' sophisticated sophisms, there is sex. An eroticism which is that fundamental *jouissance* of the text in Romanticism is found in Novalis's work. For Novalis, love and philosophy are aspects of the same mystery. 'It is with love as with philosophy', he writes (*Pollen*, 57). He evokes the *eroticism* of philosophy, something which Plato may have understood subconsciously, but which Novalis brings into the foreground:

35 Quoted in James M. Clark & John V. Skinner: *Meister Eckhart*, London 1953, 151

In the essential sense, philosophizing is – a caress – a testimony to the inner love of reflection, the absolute delight of wisdom. (53)

For Novalis, the highest form of love is spiritual, of course. In this he is in harmony with those other great poets of love, such as Dante Alighieri, Francesco Petrarch, Guido Guinicelli, Guido Cavalcanti and Bernard de Ventadour. For the mediæval troubadours and *stilnovisti*, human love was transcended in stature and significance by spiritual love. In personal terms, this meant that the human, flesh–and–blood beloved, Petrarch's Laura, Dante's Beatrice, Novalis' Sophie, was surpassed, spiritually, and even transcended physically in some cases, by the figure of the Virgin Mary. Novalis too, like Dante and Petrarch, raised the Mother of God above his Sophie as a beloved.

By absolute will power, love can be gradually transmuted into religion.[36]

This is a familiar pose with (usually male) poets, this worldly renunciation in favour of religious love. 'What I feel for Sophie', Novalis wrote, 'is religion, not love' (ib., 295).

Friedrich Nietzsche had a theory that the more tragic tragedy becomes, the more sensual it becomes. In other words, tragedy has a sensual dimension which increases as the sense of tragedy increases. William Shakespeare's tragedies are his most erotic works. Think of the erotic entanglements of love and death in *Macbeth,* or *King Lear.* Novalis too spoke of the erotic quality of intensity and absolutism. Power is an aphrodisiac, it is said: the powerful people are those who can go to extremes. Tragic characters go to extremes – Macbeth, Beatrice, Othello – they push against their ontological boundaries. They practice a kind of absolutism or extremism that seems particularly Romantic. Novalis notes the sensuality of power and extremism in his fragments, as when he claims:

All absolute sensation is religious. (197)

Tragic power and political power is sexual and seductive, and so is

36 Novalis, *Works* (Minor) II, 299

magical power. Novalis writes:

Magic is like art – to wilfully use the sensual realm. (119)

Magicians throughout history have been erotic figures: Aleister Crowley, Georg Gurdjieff, Merlin, Paracelsus. The eroticism of magic is obvious: witchcraft, for instance, was and is regarded very much in sexual terms. Witchcraft was a heresy, certainly, that disturbed the Church for religious reasons, but many of the accusations brought against witchcraft were of a sexual nature.

More 'ordinary' – that is, bourgeois, heterosexual, traditional – are the views of Novalis on love such as this:

Every beloved object is the focus of a paradise... One touches heaven, when one touches a human body. (30, 59)

This neatly summarizes the links between love and religion that have been described throughout history, from the Biblical *Song of Songs* onwards. Novalis says that you touch heaven when you touch a body. This is what the troubadours said, that making love was heavenly, that to enter a woman was to enter heaven. William Shakespeare said it, John Donne said it, John Keats said it, and Robert Graves said it in the British poetic tradition; Sappho and C.P. Cavafy said it in the Greek tradition; Ovid, Dante Alighieri and Giuseppe Ungaretti said it in the Italian tradition; Novalis, Joseph Freiherr von Eichendorff, Ludwig von Tieck and Rainer Maria Rilke said it in the German tradition; Alexander Pushkin, Fyodor Tyutchev, Arseny Tarkovsky and Anna Akhmatova said it in the Russian tradition.

Not all of Novalis' eroticism was cerebral, philosophic and 'ideal-istic'. He produced obvious eroticism at times, the sensual love of a beloved which centres on the body:

Wonderful powers of the bodily appearance – the beautiful lineaments – the form – the voice – the complexion – the musculature and elasticity – the eyes, the senses of touch, of feeling – the outer nature – the angles – the closed–off spaces – the darkness – the veil. Through the selection of clothing the body becomes yet more mystical. (116)

In Novalis' *Hymns To the Night*, the night itself is a vast, erotic, maternal, deep, dazzling space, the place of Henry Vaughan's 'deep, but dazzling darkness', the darkness of occultism and præternaturalism, the night that is the Goddess, the Mother Night of mythology, the Gnostic Night which is embodied in the Goddess Sophia, Wisdom, the night of shamanic flights. Rainer Maria Rilke in his *Duino Elegies*, wrote lyrically of this erotic night that whirls about humans and is full of angels:

> But, oh, the nights – those nights when the infinite wind
> eats at our faces! Who is immune to the night, to Night,
> ever–subtle, deceiving? Hardest of all, to the lonely,
> Night, is she gentler to lovers?[37]

Rainer Maria Rilke's poetic night is a bliss space which is clearly the external metaphor or image of the poet's inner space. It is a space of the invisible, where the Rilkean 'Open' can flourish. Novalis' night is similarly mythical:

> Downward I turn
> Toward the holy unspeakable
> Mysterious Night
> …The great wings of the spirit lift you aloft
> And fill us with joy
> Dark and unspeakable,
> Secret, as you yourself are,
> Joy that foreshadows
> A heaven to us.
> …Heavenly as flashing stars
> In each vastness
> Appear the infinite eyes
> Which the Night opens in us.[38]

Novalis, in his opening section of the *Hymns To the Night*, begins with that universal journey of heroes: into the underworld. It is a primary myth, this descent. In mythology it is often to Hell: Dante, Orpheus, Jesus, and Isis: they descend into the underworld. Of course, by Novalis' epoch, this nocturnal realm was identified with the inner

37 R. Rilke: *Duino Elegies*, tr. Stephen Cohn, Carcanet Press 1989, 21
38 Novalis: *Pollen*, 138–140

spaces. Novalis knew that the descent into an external, mythic space was the expression of an inner, psychic descent.

When he has made the shamanic journey into the unknown, invisible, dark realm, he finds... what? His beloved, his Muse, the Queen of the Night: veritably, the Black Goddess:

> Praise the Queen of the World
> The highest messenger
> Of the holy world,
> The one who nurtures
> Holy love.
> You come, Beloved –,
> The Night is here –
> My soul is enchanted –
> The earthly day is past
> And you are mine again.
> I gaze into your deep dark eyes
> And see nothing but love and ecstasy.
> We sink upon the altar of Night
> Upon the soft bed –
> The veil drops
> And kindled by your heated touch
> The flame of the sweet offering
> Glows. (140-1)

Novalis here describes the basic story or myth of Western culture: the descent and return, the journey to fundamental ontologies, the resacralization of life, symbolized by a spiritual union expressed in erotic terms. At the heart of the *Hymnen an die Nacht* is this erotic–spiritual union, an ecstatic fusion of dualities. It is also a poetic expression of lust, of masculinist desire. For, simply, the poet goes into the Night and he makes loves to it.

In Novalis' 1800 poem, despite the Christian and theological aspects of the work, the feminine, magical dimension is continually exalted. For Novalis, the Night is a womb out of which the Son of Light, Jesus, is born; but also, our era, the Christian epoch, is born from Mother Night. Novalis uses the typical mechanisms of shamanism – the night flight or spiritual journey – as a mythic descent and return. In section three of *Hymns to the Night,* his soul soars over the world, in the typical fashion of archaic shamanism, which is the basis of all religion:

You night raptures,
Heavenly slumbers came over me
The scene itself gently rose higher – my unbound, newborn
Soul soared over the scene. The hill became a dust cloud
and through the cloud I saw the clear features of my Beloved –
In her eyes rested Eternity… (143)

Although he sees the mythic Night as Christian, a gathering darkness after the Light or Day of Greece, Novalis continually emphasizes the feminine, maternal aspects of this mythical Night. Novalis' Night, like Rainer Maria Rilke's, is a supremely female space: 'She bears *you* – motherly', he writes (143);

The dark ocean's
Blue depths
Were a Goddess' womb.

There is much idealism in this view of a feminized soul-space, a mythic 'dreamtime' over which the Goddess presides. The upsurge of hope in the *Hymns To the Night* is very powerful:

And into heaven's
Infinite distance
Filled with the lustrous world
Into the heart of the highest spaces,
The soul of the world withdrew
With her powers
To wait for the dawn
Of new days
And the higher destiny of the world. (150-1)

By the end of the poem, the transition is made, from the dark, maternal, feminine realm of Night to the bright, rational, masculine realm of Day or Light. 'We sink into the Father's heart', writes the poet, in the last line (159). But it is an ambiguous ending, for the new form of the feminine, the Virgin Mary, is not the erotic Black Goddess of ancient times.

Novalis describes the basic emotional displacement of the psychoanalysis of childhood: the movement of the child away from the mother towards the father; from intuition to ratiocination; from emotion to reason; from dependency to independence, from femininity to masculinity; from immaturity to maturity; from the semiotic realm to the symbolic realm (the Law of the Father).

Novalis simply trades in the usual poetic fare: the associations of darkness with the feminine, light with the masculine, and so on. He employs the age-old dichotomies of Western culture, where, after a night of ecstasy, the Night is renounced in favour of the Day. It is familiar rhetoric. Novalis, though, raises it to new heights because of his energy and idealism. *Hymns To the Night* is an exuberant poetic sequence, shot through and powered by flashes of inspiration and enthusiasm. It is a poem that exists all on its own. There is nothing else quite like it – not in German Romanticism, nor in poetry throughout history. It combines elements of the theological exegesis, the courtly *canso*, the philosophical tract, utopian and idealistic mysticism, and a fervent lyrical poetry.

Hymnen an die Nacht is a poem that embellishes the norms of Western culture – heterosexuality, theology, Christianity, and philosophy without much developing them or questioning them. It is an uncritical poem, which re-states what is already known – and felt – about Western culture. Ambiguity and doubt are not high in the poetic mix: *Hymnen an die Nacht* is a mystical poem, and about the certainty of the mystical experience. After their ecstasy, mystics feel utterly sure of their faith, their God, their duty, their life. They trust their mystical ecstasy, as one must trust one's own experiences in life. Romanticism, as we have seen, is founded on subjectivity. The Romantic poets, whether of France, Germany, Britain, America or Italy, unfailingly trust their own experiences. Indeed, artists must. Novalis' *Hymns To the Night* is constructed out of the basic, unshakeable faith in the poetic self.

❦

Novalis continues to be read, as do Heinrich Heine, Johann Wolgang von Goethe, both Schlegels, Friedrich Schiller and Friedrich Hölderlin. There is a richness in poets such as Goethe and Novalis that endures. Glyn Hughes writes of Novalis:

> The sustaining interest in the reading of Novalis's works is the sense of contact with a mind of visionary intensity and total commitment. The poetic achievement is in the momentary glimpses of ideal reality: what, in other contexts, we

should call epiphanies. (61)

Novalis' *Hymns To the Night* articulates the rebirth at the heart of Romanticism, that self–invention which always goes to the heart of life by way of speaking of fundamental experiences – of love, death, birth and rebirth. From the womb of the Virgin Mother the shining self is reborn. Novalis' poetics, like those of Johann Wolfgang von Goethe, Friedrich Hölderlin, Heinrich Heine or Friedrich Schlegel, are those of a spiritual rebirth, a resacralization of life, a renaissance of life, in short. This is the goal of not just the Romantic poets, but of most poets throughout history.

Bibliography

BY NOVALIS

Recommended books are marked with an asterisk.

*Novalis Schriften. Die Werke Friedrichs von Hardenberg*ed. Richard Samuel,
    Hans-Joachim Mähl & Gerhard Schulz, Kohlhammer, Stuttgart, 1960-88 *
Pollen and Fragments: Selected Poetry and Prose, tr. Arthur Versluis, Phanes
    Press, Grand Rapids, 1989 *
Hymns to the Night and Other Selected Writings, tr. Charles E. Passage, Bobbs-
    Merrill Company, Indianapolis, 1960
Hymns to the Night, Treacle Press, New York, NY, 1978 *
Novalis: Fichte Studies, ed. J. Kneller, Cambridge University Press, Cam-bridge,
    2003
Notes For a Romantic Encyclopedia, tr. D. Wood, State University of New York
    Press, New York, 2007

ON NOVALIS

Gwendolyn Bays. *The Orphic Vision: Seer Poets from Novalis to Rimbaud*
    University of Nebraska Press, Lincoln, 1964 *
G. Birrell. *The Boundless Presence: Space and Time In the Literary Fairy Tales of
    Novalis and Tieck*, 1979
K. Calhoun. *Fatherland: Novalis, Freud and the Discipline of Romance*, 1992
Henri Clemens Birven. *Novalis, Magus der Romantik*, Schwab, Büdingen, 1959
Manfred Dick. *Die Entwicklung des Gedankens der Poesie in den Fragmenten des
    Novalis*, Bouvier, Bonn, 1967, 223-77
B. Donehower, ed. *The Birth of Novalis*, State University of New York Press, New
    York, 2007
Richard Faber. *Novalis: die Phantasie an die Macht*, Metzler, Stuttgart 1970
Walter Feilchenfeld. *Der Einfluss Jacob Böhmes auf Novalis*, Eberia, Berlin, 1922

Sara Frierichsmeyer. *The Androgyne In Early German Romanticism: Friedrich Schlegel, Novalis and the Metaphysics of Love* Bern, New York, 1983
Curt Grutzmacher. *Novalis und Philippe Otto Runge*, Eidos, Munich 1964
Theodor Haering. *Novalis als Philosoph*, Kohlhammer, Stuttgart, 1954
Bruce Haywood. *The Veil of Imagery: A Study of the Poetic Works of Friedrich von Hardenburg*, Harvard University Press, Cambridge, Mass., 1959
Frederick Heibel. *Novalis: German Poet, European Thinker, Christian Mystic* AMS, New York, 1969
L. Johns. *The Art of Recollection In Jena Romanticism* Niemeyer, Tübingen, 2002
Alice Kuzniar. *Delayed Endings: Nonclosure In Novalis and Hölderlin*, University of Georgia Press, Athens, 1987
Géza von Molnar. *Novalis's Fichte Studies*, Mouton, The Hague 1970
—. *Romantic Vision, Ethical Context: Novalis and Artistic Autonomy* University of Minnesota Press, Minneapolis 1987
Bruno Müller. *Novalis – der dichter als Mittler*, Lang, Bern, 1984
John Neubauer. *Bifocal Vision: Novalis's Philosophy of Nature and Disease*, Chapel Hill 1972
—. *Novalis*, 1980
I. Nikolova. *Complementary Modes of Representation In Keats, Novalis and Shelley*, Peter Lang, New York, 2001
W. O'Brien. *Novalis*, 1995
Nicholas Saul. *History and Poetry In Novalis and In the Tradition of the German Enlightenment*, Institute of Germanic Studies, 1984
Karl Heinz Volkmann-Schluck. "Novalis' magischer Idealismus", *Die deutsche Romantik*, ed. Hans Steffen, 1967, 45-53

OTHERS

Ernst Behler. *German Romantic Literary Theory*, Cambridge University Press, 1993 *
Ernst Benz. *The Mystical Sources of German Romantic Philosophy* tr. B. Reynolds & E. Paul, Pickwick, Allison Park, 1983
Richard Brinkmann, ed. *Romantik in Deutschland*, Metzler, Stuttgart, 1978
Manfred Brown. *The Shape of German Romanticism*, Cornell University Press, Ithaca, 1979
Hans Eichner. *Friedrich Schlegel*, Twayne, New York, 1970
R.W. Ewton. *The Literary Theory of A.W. Schlegel* Mouthon, The Hague, 1971
Michael Hamburger. *Reason and Energy: Studies In German Literature* Weidenfeld & Nicolson, 1970 *
Heinrich Heine. *The Complete Poems of Heinrich Heine* tr. Hal Draper, Suhrkamp/ Insel, Boston, 1982
—. *The North Sea*, tr. Vernon Watkins, Faber, 1955
Friedrich Hölderlin. *Poems and Fragments*, tr. Michael Hamburger, Routledge & Kegan Paul, 1966
Glyn Tegai Hughes. *Romantic German Literature*, Edward Arnold, 1979 *
Philippe Lacoue-Labarthe & Jean-Luc Nancy, eds. *The Literary Absolute: The*

Theory of Literature In German Romanticism ,State University of New York
   Press, Albany, 1988
D. Mahoney. *The Critical Fortunes of a Romantic Novel,* 1994
Ritchie Robertson. *Heine*, Peter Halban, 1988
Helmut Schanze. *Romantik und Aufklärung, Unterschungen zu Friedrich Schlegel
   und Novalis*, Carl, Nürnberg, 1966
—. ed. *Friedrich Schlegel und die Kunstheorie Seiner Zeit* Wissenschaftliche
   Buchgesellschaft, Darmstadt, 1985
Elizabeth Sewell. *The Orphic Voice: Poetry and Natural History* ,Routledge,
   1961*

WEBSITES

Aquarium	novalis.autorenverzeichnis.de
Novalis Gesellschaft	novalis-gesellschaft.de
International Novalis Society	ula.org/s/or/en

Arseny Tarkovsky

Life, Life

Selected Poems

Arseny Tarkovsky is the neglected Russian poet, father of the acclaimed film director Andrei Tarkovsky. This new book gathers together many of Tarkovsky's most lyrical and heartfelt poems, in Virginia Rounding's new, clear translations. Many of Tarkovsky's poems appeared in his son's films, such as *Mirror, Stalker, Nostalghia* and *The Sacrifice*. There is an introduction by Rounding, and a bibliography of both Arseny and Andrei Tarkovsky.

Illustrated. Bibliography and notes.
ISBN 9781816171144 Pbk   ISBN 9781861712660 Hbk

In the Dim Void

Samuel Beckett's Late Trilogy:
Company, Ill Seen, Ill Said and *Worstward Ho*

by Gregory Johns

This book discusses the luminous beauty and dense, rigorous poetry of Samuel Beckett's late works, *Company, Ill Seen, Ill Said* and *Worstward Ho*. Gregory Johns looks back over Beckett's long writing career, charting the development from the *Molloy-Malone Dies-Unnamable* trilogy through the 'fizzles' of the 1960s to the elegiac lyricism of the *Company* series. Johns compares the trilogy with late plays such as *Ghosts, Footfalls* and *Rockaby*.

Bibliography, notes. Illustrated. 120pp
ISBN 9781861712974 Pbk and ISBN 9781861712608 Hbk
9781861713407 E-book

CRESCENT MOON PUBLISHING

web: www.crmoon.com e-mail: cresmopub@yahoo.co.uk

ARTS, PAINTING, SCULPTURE

The Art of Andy Goldsworthy
Andy Goldsworthy: Touching Nature
Andy Goldsworthy in Close-Up
Andy Goldsworthy: Pocket Guide
Andy Goldsworthy In America
Land Art: A Complete Guide
The Art of Richard Long
Richard Long: Pocket Guide
Land Art In the UK
Land Art in Close-Up
Land Art In the U.S.A.
Land Art: Pocket Guide
Installation Art in Close-Up
Minimal Art and Artists In the 1960s and After
Colourfield Painting
Land Art DVD, TV documentary
Andy Goldsworthy DVD, TV documentary
The Erotic Object: Sexuality in Sculpture From Prehistory to the Present Day
Sex in Art: Pornography and Pleasure in Painting and Sculpture
Postwar Art
Sacred Gardens: The Garden in Myth, Religion and Art
Glorification: Religious Abstraction in Renaissance and 20th Century Art
Early Netherlandish Painting
Leonardo da Vinci
Piero della Francesca
Giovanni Bellini
Fra Angelico: Art and Religion in the Renaissance
Mark Rothko: The Art of Transcendence
Frank Stella: American Abstract Artist
Jasper Johns
Brice Marden
Alison Wilding: The Embrace of Sculpture
Vincent van Gogh: Visionary Landscapes
Eric Gill: Nuptials of God
Constantin Brancusi: Sculpting the Essence of Things
Max Beckmann
Caravaggio
Gustave Moreau
Egon Schiele: Sex and Death In Purple Stockings
Delizioso Fotografico Fervore: Works In Process 1
Sacro Cuore: Works In Process 2
The Light Eternal: J.M.W. Turner
The Madonna Glorified: Karen Arthurs

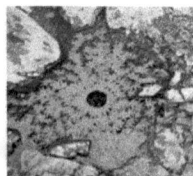

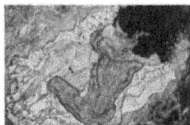

LITERATURE

J.R.R. Tolkien: The Books, The Films, The Whole Cultural Phenomenon
J.R.R. Tolkien: Pocket Guide
Tolkien's Heroic Quest
The *Earthsea* Books of Ursula Le Guin
Beauties, Beasts and Enchantment: Classic French Fairy Tales
German Popular Stories by the Brothers Grimm
Philip Pullman and *His Dark Materials*
Sexing Hardy: Thomas Hardy and Feminism
Thomas Hardy's *Tess of the d'Urbervilles*
Thomas Hardy's *Jude the Obscure*
Thomas Hardy: The Tragic Novels
Love and Tragedy: Thomas Hardy
The Poetry of Landscape in Hardy

Wessex Revisited: Thomas Hardy and John Cowper Powys
Wolfgang Iser: Essays and Interviews
Petrarch, Dante and the Troubadours
Maurice Sendak and the Art of Children's Book Illustration
Andrea Dworkin
Cixous, Irigaray, Kristeva: The *Jouissance* of French Feminism
Julia Kristeva: Art, Love, Melancholy, Philosophy, Semiotics and Psychoanalysis
Hélène Cixous I Love You: The *Jouissance* of Writing
Luce Irigaray: Lips, Kissing, and the Politics of Sexual Difference
Peter Redgrove: Here Comes the Flood
Peter Redgrove: Sex-Magic-Poetry-Cornwall

Lawrence Durrell: Between Love and Death, East and West
Love, Culture & Poetry: Lawrence Durrell
Cavafy: Anatomy of a Soul
German Romantic Poetry: Goethe, Novalis, Heine, Hölderlin
Feminism and Shakespeare
Shakespeare: Love, Poetry & Magic
The Passion of D.H. Lawrence
D.H. Lawrence: Symbolic Landscapes
D.H. Lawrence: Infinite Sensual Violence
Rimbaud: Arthur Rimbaud and the Magic of Poetry
The Ecstasies of John Cowper Powys
Sensualism and Mythology: The Wessex Novels of John Cowper Powys
Amorous Life: John Cowper Powys and the Manifestation of Affectivity (H.W. Fawkner)
Postmodern Powys: New Essays on John Cowper Powys (Joe Boulter)
Rethinking Powys: Critical Essays on John Cowper Powys
Paul Bowles & Bernardo Bertolucci
Rainer Maria Rilke

Joseph Conrad: *Heart of Darkness*
In the Dim Void: Samuel Beckett
Samuel Beckett Goes into the Silence
André Gide: Fiction and Fervour

Jackie Collins and the Blockbuster Novel
Blinded By Her Light: The Love-Poetry of Robert Graves
The Passion of Colours: Travels In Mediterranean Lands
Poetic Forms

POETRY

Ursula Le Guin: Walking In Cornwall
Peter Redgrove: Here Comes The Flood
Peter Redgrove: Sex-Magic-Poetry-Cornwall
Dante: Selections From the Vita Nuova
Petrarch, Dante and the Troubadours
William Shakespeare: Sonnets
William Shakespeare: Complete Poems
Blinded By Her Light: The Love-Poetry of Robert Graves
Emily Dickinson: Selected Poems
Emily Brontë: Poems
Thomas Hardy: Selected Poems
Percy Bysshe Shelley: Poems
John Keats: Selected Poems
John Keats: Poems of 1820
D.H. Lawrence: Selected Poems
Edmund Spenser: Poems
Edmund Spenser: Amoretti
John Donne: Poems
Henry Vaughan: Poems
Sir Thomas Wyatt: Poems
Robert Herrick: Selected Poems
Rilke: Space, Essence and Angels in the Poetry of Rainer Maria Rilke
Rainer Maria Rilke: Selected Poems
Friedrich Hölderlin: Selected Poems
Arseny Tarkovsky: Selected Poems
Arthur Rimbaud: Selected Poems
Arthur Rimbaud: A Season in Hell
Arthur Rimbaud and the Magic of Poetry
Novalis: Hymns To the Night
German Romantic Poetry
Paul Verlaine: Selected Poems
Elizaethan Sonnet Cycles
D.J. Enright: By-Blows
Jeremy Reed: Brigitte's Blue Heart
Jeremy Reed: Claudia Schiffer's Red Shoes
Gorgeous Little Orpheus
Radiance: New Poems
Crescent Moon Book of Nature Poetry
Crescent Moon Book of Love Poetry
Crescent Moon Book of Mystical Poetry
Crescent Moon Book of Elizabethan Love Poetry
Crescent Moon Book of Metaphysical Poetry
Crescent Moon Book of Romantic Poetry
Pagan America: New American Poetry

MEDIA, CINEMA, FEMINISM and CULTURAL STUDIES

J.R.R. Tolkien: The Books, The Films, The Whole Cultural Phenomenon
J.R.R. Tolkien: Pocket Guide
The *Lord of the Rings* Movies: Pocket Guide
The Cinema of Hayao Miyazaki
Hayao Miyazaki: *Princess Mononoke*: Pocket Movie Guide
Hayao Miyazaki: *Spirited Away*: Pocket Movie Guide
Tim Burton : Hallowe'en For Hollywood
Ken Russell
Ken Russell: *Tommy*: Pocket Movie Guide
The Ghost Dance: The Origins of Religion
The Peyote Cult
Cixous, Irigaray, Kristeva: The *Jouissance* of French Feminism
Julia Kristeva: Art, Love, Melancholy, Philosophy, Semiotics and Psychoanalysis
Luce Irigaray: Lips, Kissing, and the Politics of Sexual Difference
Hélène Cixous I Love You: The *Jouissance* of Writing
Andrea Dworkin
'Cosmo Woman': The World of Women's Magazines
Women in Pop Music
HomeGround: The Kate Bush Anthology
Discovering the Goddess (Geoffrey Ashe)
The Poetry of Cinema
The Sacred Cinema of Andrei Tarkovsky
Andrei Tarkovsky: Pocket Guide
Andrei Tarkovsky: *Mirror*: Pocket Movie Guide
Andrei Tarkovsky: *The Sacrifice*: Pocket Movie Guide
Walerian Borowczyk: Cinema of Erotic Dreams
Jean-Luc Godard: The Passion of Cinema
Jean-Luc Godard: *Hail Mary*: Pocket Movie Guide
Jean-Luc Godard: *Contempt*: Pocket Movie Guide
Jean-Luc Godard: *Pierrot le Fou*: Pocket Movie Guide
John Hughes and Eighties Cinema
Ferris Bueller's Day Off: Pocket Movie Guide
Jean-Luc Godard: Pocket Guide
The Cinema of Richard Linklater
Liv Tyler: Star In Ascendance
Blade Runner and the Films of Philip K. Dick
Paul Bowles and Bernardo Bertolucci
Media Hell: Radio, TV and the Press
An Open Letter to the BBC
Detonation Britain: Nuclear War in the UK
Feminism and Shakespeare
Wild Zones: Pornography, Art and Feminism
Sex in Art: Pornography and Pleasure in Painting and Sculpture
Sexing Hardy: Thomas Hardy and Feminism

The Light Eternal is a model monograph, an exemplary job. The subject matter of the book is beautifully organised and dead on beam. (Lawrence Durrell)
It is amazing for me to see my work treated with such passion and respect. (Andrea Dworkin)

CRESCENT MOON PUBLISHING
P.O. Box 1312, Maidstone, Kent, ME14 5XU, Great Britain. www.crmoon.com

cresmopub@yahoo.co.uk   www.crescentmoon.org.uk